KNOW YOUR BIBLE SERIES

8

**THESSALONIANS
GALATIANS
CORINTHIANS
ROMANS**

ROY L. SMITH

ABINGDON PRESS
NASHVILLE

Thessalonians, Galatians, Corinthians, Romans

INTRODUCTION

There has been a disposition on the part of modern Christians to idealize those first-century Christians, to picture them as being people of rare spiritual achievements, unusual piety, unimpeachable morals, and rich religious insights. We are frequently urged to return to the high devotion of the early Church as though the first century were the golden age of Christianity.

That the first disciples were brave souls no one can deny. It requires a rare degree of courage to enable one to set out upon an uncharted sea with an untried faith, and those daring spirits did so with an intrepidity that is amazing. But even when they have been given all credit for their religious pioneering, still the simple truth is that they were not the unsullied characters we have sometimes supposed they were.

A fearless investigation of the New Testament reveals the fact that the early Church was rent by many controversies, that there were many sharp divisions among the believers, that the membership was made up of people who were spiritually immature, and that much actual immorality found its way into the organization at one time or another. Those first-century Christians were easily led off by fanatics, really heroic on occasions but also often a problem.

The student can well afford to bear in mind that we are investigating some personal letters. We have called them "books" so long that we are apt to forget that they were, actually, personal communications designed as private letters to intimate friends, and must be studied as such. Although Paul very evidently gave much thought to the composition of these letters, he did not set out in any case to write a book on theology. Instead he deals with particular problems of particular congregations, and in the course of much writing sometimes makes statements which seem to conflict and which are difficult to reconcile.

For some reason which is not quite clear, Paul seems to have employed a secretary to do much of the work of actual writing. This was an art that called for no small amount of skill, and writing materials were expensive. But in each case he signed the letters personally, and in at least three instances makes some special mention of the fact (I Corinthians 16:21; Colossians 4:18;

3

II Thessalonians 3:17). In one or two cases, in order to save the labor and expense of making duplicate copies, he gave specific directions that more than one congregation should read what he had written (I Thessalonians 5:27; Colossians 4:16).

The Christian worship services of the day were informal gatherings without any fixed "order of worship." They were actually little more than social gatherings of half-instructed people who came together for conference and counsel. If any wandering preacher happened to be in the city, he talked with them and gave them the benefit of whatever advice or knowledge he might have had. To such meetings Paul's letters were read, and they were heard with great interest.

On one occasion Paul admitted very candidly that he was not a great success as a public speaker (I Corinthians 2:1), but even his enemies had to admit that he was an effective letter writer (II Corinthians 10:10), and it is through his private correspondence that he has made his great contribution to the thought and life of the Christian Church down through the centuries. It is an interesting fact that Paul is the only great preacher of the times whose sermons are preserved for us in letter form. It would be of great help to us if we could have some of Barnabas' letters or excerpts from the sermons of Apollos, in order to compare them with Paul's writings, but none such exist as far as we know. The fact that Paul's letters have been preserved for us is an eloquent testimony to the high regard in which the Apostle was held by the first-century Church.

It is unfortunate that we do not have all of Paul's letters. No one knows how many he actually wrote, but we do know of several that have been lost (I Corinthians 5:9; II Corinthians 2:4; 7:8), and there were probably others of which no trace remains.

We turn now to one of the most fascinating excursions in all the field of Bible study. Try to imagine, if you can, that you have suddenly come upon a packet of old letters, and that by studying them with great care, noting at times the delicate shades of meaning resident in a single word, the conditions of the times out of which they came, the people to whom they were addressed, and the purpose they were expected to serve, you are trying to get an understanding of their author.

Roy L. Smith

4

Paul Launches the New Testament

1 What is the New Testament?

It is a collection of sacred writings produced by the early Christian Church.

2 Why is it called the New Testament?

The Jews often called themselves "the people of the covenant," because they believed God had entered into an agreement with their fathers (Genesis 17:2 ff.; Exodus 24:1-8) whereby the nation became God's people and he became their God. They sometimes called themselves the "children" of the covenant. This agreement between God and the nation constituted a distinguishing mark by which they were set off from all other peoples of the ancient world.

There came a time, however, when one of their greatest prophets predicted that the covenant would be superseded by another agreement (Jeremiah 31:31-33); and the Christians believed that the ministry of Jesus, together with his death and resurrection, constituted this new agreement, or covenant (I Corinthians 11:25; Hebrews 8:6-13). They believed that by Jesus' death God entered into a new arrangement with mankind. This new period they knew by several names, but one fact characterized it—they were no longer under the Jewish law, but had entered into an agreement which promised freedom (Galatians 4:24-26). The first Christian books which were assembled by the Church were called "the books of the new covenant," or "testament," which in time was shortened to "New Testament."

3 What is the difference between "new covenant" and "New Testament"?

The name "New Testament" came into popular English use somewhat by accident. The Greek word for "covenant" was also the word for "will," or "testament." When the scriptures were translated from the Greek into the Latin (A.D. 404), God was thought of somewhat as one would think of a man who was disposing of his property by bequest. Having made one will, he changes the conditions for some reason and makes a new one. The first covenant was thought of as the first will, and the Christian "covenant" as the second. Thus it happened that the Christian scriptures came to be called the "New Testament."

4 Did these writings produce the Christian Church?

No. On the contrary, the Christian Church produced the New Testament.

5 Was there a Church before there was a New Testament?

Yes, many years before. The Christian Church was born on an occasion called "Pentecost," about A.D. 28, some seven weeks after the crucifixion of Jesus. From the moment of its inception it began making a rapid growth, and many congregations had been established before a single line of Christian writing came into existence. It was spreading across the earth at a rapid rate before the first Christian book was written, and was a world organization long before any official action was taken designating the New Testament as being "inspired scripture."

6 Where did all this happen?

Generally speaking, it may be said to have taken place along the eastern shores of the Mediterranean. This was a part of the Roman Empire, but culturally speaking it was Greek. The Greek language was used everywhere, Greek learning pervaded the universities, and Greek manners dominated the life of the land. It was a world in which learning was held in high respect, in which many books on a variety of subjects were in circulation, and in which much reading was done. All this had a very profound influence upon the infant Church born at Pentecost.

7 What was Pentecost?

Numerous annual feasts were held by the Jews of the first century, all of which were closely associated with the ancestral faith of the nation. The most conspicuous of these, of course, was the Passover, which celebrated the escape of the Hebrews from Egyptian bondage under the leadership of Moses (Exodus 12; Deuteronomy 16:1-8). Fifty days later there occurred a single-day festival called the Feast of Weeks, which celebrated the close of the harvest. Because it was celebrated on the fiftieth day following the beginning of the Feast of the Passover, the Greek word "Pentecost" (meaing "fiftieth") was adopted as the name of the feast, somewhat as "the Fourth" has come to mean "Independence Day" to the people of the United States.

8 **What connection did Pentecost have with the Church?**

On the day of Pentecost following the crucifixion of Jesus—which occurred on the even of the Passover—a considerable number of Christians were gathered in Jerusalem. In the midst of their meeting astonishing things took place (Acts 2:1-4) which convinced all who witnessed them that God had revealed himself in a miraculous way. Under the inspiration of the occasion Peter, the leader of the Christians, preached a sermon so forceful and persuasive that three thousand converts were enlisted in the movement. Out from that meeting the Christians went to preach the new faith (the new covenant), and so effective were they that new congregations began to form soon after Pentecost in widely separated sections of the empire. Because of the events witnessed on the day of Pentecost, Christian historians have referred to it as the birthday of the Church.

9 **Who were the Christians?**

The first disciples of Jesus were all Jews, and—with the exception of Judas—the betrayer, who was a Judean—all were Galileans. It is reported that "certain Greeks" became interested in Jesus and his ministry (John 12:20-23), but there is nothing to indicate that they ever became his followers. It is even possible that Jesus preached to many non-Jews and that many of them showed marked interest in his message (Mark 7:24-30; Matthew 8:5-13; Luke 7:2-16), but none became members of the Christian community so far as we know. All Christians were Jews at the outset of the movement.

10 **Did these Christians have any Christian writings?**

None whatever. There is no evidence in the New Testament that a single line of Christian writing existed among them. As a matter of fact, there was an expectation among the Christians which would have discouraged the production of any writings.

11 What was that expectation?

Following Jesus' death and resurrection he appeared on numerous occasions to various groups and individuals (Acts 1:3). Conversations held at such times, together with some scattered remarks and the amazing fact of the resurrection, gave rise to a belief among Christians that he was soon to return and set up a visible kingdom, perhaps political in form, which he would rule and which would bring all the earth under his authority.

12 How did this affect the writing of scripture?

A group of people who expected Jesus' speedy return would see little value in writing down any record of his early life. His visible, tangible, personal presence would be so completely sufficient that they would feel no need of any Christian writings or records. Added to the foregoing was the fact that his whole life had been a miracle about which men's thinking was still very hazy. They could not comprehend it, and people do not usually begin writing until they begin to understand. Perhaps most important of all considerations was the stupendous fact upon which all Christian confidence and faith rested.

13 What was that fact?

The great historic event about which the Church grew up—the resurrection of Jesus. This was the very core of Christian belief. About it all other facts and elements of faith revolved. No matter how the Christians might disagree about other matters, on the fact of the Resurrection there was unanimity of opinion.

14 What constituted the importance of the Resurrection?

It was the bedrock of the whole Christian movement. Every Christian believed that Jesus Christ, the prophet from Nazareth, who had been crucified by Pilate and entombed in Joseph's tomb, had walked forth from that tomb alive, and that he continued alive in spirit and in fact. Indeed, they believed that his spirit communicated with them, inspired them, supplemented their knowledge, guided them, and actually lived with them. Everywhere they went preaching, they declared that "he who was dead is alive again." The greatest of all the Christian evangelists one time said, "If Jesus' resurrection is not a fact, then we have no gospel to preach" (I Corinthians 15:14). All other facts concerning the life of Jesus were remembered if, or because, they contributed somewhat to an understanding or appreciation of this stupendous and amazing act of God—the raising of Jesus from the dead—which marked the end of one era and the beginning of another. The theme of all the preaching of the first-century Christian Church was the resurrection of Jesus. Those first preachers had but one text: "He has risen." Paul declared that he was determined to know nothing among them beyond the single fact of Jesus' death, but that took on its significance because of the Resurrection.

15 What does all this mean?

It means that the earthly life and ministry of Jesus were interesting to the first-century Church only as they might throw light upon this crowning experience of the Resurrection. Incidents out of his life and sayings out of his teachings were told and retold among the Christians because they explained in some way the character and work of One who had been exalted by God and who was to become "the judge of the living and the dead." The gospel which the first-century Christians preached was, for the most part, that single event which marked him as the triumphant Spirit whom the grave could not hold. The resurrection story is the heart and core of each of the Gospels.

16 Did the Resurrection produce the Christian Church?

Without a doubt. Modern Christianity ascribes much importance to the life and works of Jesus, and this is proper. But the thing that captured the imagination and won the loyalty of that first-century Christian community was the Resurrection—the fact that Jesus had risen triumphantly over the grave. Events in his life took on new meaning because they were events in the life of a man who had risen from the dead. This unparalleled fact converted people to the belief that Jesus was the Son of God. It drove them to ask, "Why did he die?" By the time the four Gospels came into their final form, the death of Jesus was the major problem in Christian thinking. They reasoned from the fact of his defeat of death to his divinity. Without the Resurrection, Jesus might have been forgotten within the space of a generation, in spite of any miracle he might have worked or any unusual teachings he might have given to the world. It was the Resurrection that sent those first-century Christians up and down through the world preaching the "new covenant."

17 What kind of people were those first Christians?

Among the original disciples there were a few who were of some local importance, perhaps. One of them, Matthew, had been an important Roman official in Capernaum. But for the most part they were plain people of ordinary intelligence who were unschooled in the fine points of Jewish theology or Greek philsophy. But they came under the spell of that great fact—the Resurrection—and, turning their backs on their accustomed pursuits, set out deliberately to preach the new faith founded on that fact. The original disciples seem to have given themselves over to propagating the sect; but for the most part the first Christian evangelists were merely people who, having become convinced of the significance and meaning of the resurrection of Jesus, preached their convictions as opportunity afforded while they carried on their normal vocations. Here and there, however, individuals of outstanding intellectual ability and spirituality joined themselves to the movement and contributed learning to the Christian program. A few people of modest wealth joined the fellowship. Now and then a convert was made from the ranks of the fanatical Jews to whom the Law was the supreme authority for all of life. Such a one was Paul the Apostle.

18 Who was Paul?

In spite of the fact that he is, next to Jesus himself, the most conspicuous personality in the New Testament, and the greatest single force in the New Testament, we know comparatively little about his private life. He seems to have been born a free citizen of Rome, in the city of Tarsus, about A.D. 6, though no exact dates are mentioned in the record. In addition to the fact that his father seems to have been a man of some wealth—attested by the fact that Paul went to Jerusalem for an education (Acts 22:3)—the family was evidently devout and faithful in its observance of the Jewish Law (Philippians 3:5-6; II Corinthians 11:22, Romans 4:1; 9:3; 11:1; Acts 23:6; 26:4-5; Galatians 1:14).

He was a man of towering intellectual strength who in the course of his ministry was instrumental in founding some of the most influential of the early churches, and to several of these he wrote letters which eventually became parts of the New Testament.

19   When did he live?

It is impossible to fix many exact dates in connection with the life of Paul, for he furnishes few clues in his own writings, and there are few other records available. Occasional bits of information have proved helpful, however. Herod Agrippa, for instance, a grandson of Herod the Great, who governed Palestine in Rome's behalf, died in Caesarea in A.D. 44. Toward the close of his brief career (three years), he instituted a persecution of the Christians which resulted in the martyrdom of James the brother of John (Acts 12:1-4, 19-23) and one of the disciples. Peter, another of the disciples, was imprisoned. About the same time a famine developed in Judea which resulted in great suffering among the Christians. To relieve their distress Paul and Barnabas, another Christian preacher, collected a considerable fund among the churches (Acts 11:27-30) and made a trip to Jerusalem for the purpose of delivering it into the hands of the leaders of the Church. By comparing these different events and dates historians have decided that Paul's visit must have occurred about A.D. 45 or 46.

The date of the crucifixion has been fixed as about A.D. 28, and Paul's conversion is reckoned to have occurred only a few years thereafter, perhaps A.D. 33 or 34. These, of course, are only approximate dates. Paul was a "young man" at the time of the stoning of Stephen, the first Christian martyr (Acts 7:58), but he had established some reputation among the Jews for piety, devotion, and a scrupulous observance of the Law. He was granted letters of authority (Acts 8:3; 9:2) by the leaders of the Jews, which could hardly have been possible if he had been a mere youth. On the basis of such scanty facts, historians are of the opinion that he must have been born about A.D. 6, and that he was in the neighborhood of thirty years of age at the time of his conversion. His ministry continued for some thirty years thereafter, and he seems to have died at the age of about sixty, a martyr. We must beware of assuming that these dates are exact, however.

20 How was he converted?

Beginning at Pentecost, only a few weeks following the crucifixion, the Christians charged that the Jews had killed "the Lord's anointed." This charge, together with the fact that the Christians held meetings of their own, apart from the Temple or the synagogue services of the Jews, whereat they worshiped Jesus according to their own forms, aroused among the Jews considerable opposition, which increased in fury as time went on. Finally the Christians were being attacked, beaten, stoned, and otherwise roughly handled, with feeling running very high.

Among the ringleaders of the persecution was Paul, a zealous young Pharisee who bore the name of Saul—possibly in honor of the first Hebrew king. With the energy and zeal characteristic of youth, this young man made his name a synonym for terror among Christians everywhere. He was feared with a dreadful fear wherever Christians were gathered together. Not satisfied with persecuting the Christians of Jerusalem, and hearing of the formation of a Christian community among the Jews of Damascus, he obtained permission from the Temple authorities to duplicate there the reign of terror he had instituted among the Jerusalem Christians (Acts 9:2).

At the outset of the persecutions a Christian of impressive personality had been stoned to death just outside the city, and something in the way the young man died made a very great impression on Saul, who witnessed his death (Acts 7:58). There is nothing in the Scriptures which declares it definitely, but it is generally believed that the young Pharisee was never able to escape the memory of that tragedy. At any rate it happened that the young zealot, Saul, was making a trip to Damascus intent on slaughtering Christians, and while on his way was arrested by an amazing vision during which he believed he heard the voice of Jesus calling him to account (Acts 9:3-20). With characteristic forthrightness—moved, perhaps, by his memories of the martyr Stephen—he committed himself to his new Lord and proceeded to Damascus to join himself to the Christian community there. Thus he began his career as "an apostle of Christ Jesus."

21 Why is he called both Saul and Paul?

It was not an uncommon thing for men to have two names—one a Jewish and the other a Greek or Roman name. Saul was the Hebrew name by which he seems to have been known among the Jews in Jerusalem, at least up to the time of his journey to Damascus. Outside of Palestine, however, he probably used his Roman name, or it was used by others when speaking of him. From the time he began preaching to the Gentiles he seems to have gone by the name of Paul entirely.

22 Were all Christians Jews at the time of his conversion?

They were, though some were called "Hellenists" (translated "Grecians" in the King James Version). These should not be confused with the actual Greeks, who called themselves "Hellenes."

23 Who were the Hellenists?

Both by force of circumstances, and by disposition, the Jews had become a migratory people, and settlements were to be found throughout the Roman Empire. There was considerable traffic between Jerusalem and the Jews of the rest of the world, and those living in the Greek-speaking countries were known as "Hellenists." In addition to the fact that they spoke Greek, these Jews very frequently differed from their Palestinian countrymen in their religious attitudes, being influenced in the direction of liberality by their Greek environment.

The first line of cleavage that appeared in the Christian Church was associated with these Hellenists. The first converts who flocked into the Church on the day of Pentecost under Peter's inspired preaching were those who had come to Jerusalem for the religious feasts (Acts 2:5). Before long a division arose within the Church (Acts 6:1) in which the Hellenists were pitted against the Palestinians; and Stephen, who was to become the first Christian martyr, became the leader of the Hellenist faction. After his death the Hellenists scattered, perhaps for prudential reasons, to the cities from which they had come, and thus the Christian evangel began to spread among the Greek-speaking Jews of all the world.

One fact must be kept in mind, however, and that is that they were all Jews. Those whom Paul persecuted in Jerusalem and those he proposed to persecute in Damascus were "of the household of Israel." Up to this time no Gentiles were affiliated with the movement.

24 Was Paul a Hellenist?

He was born of Jewish parent in the city of Tarsus and spoke the Greek dialect of the common people. When he arrived in Jersualem to take up his education, he was recognized among the Palestinian Jews as a Hellenist. There was then this tie between him and the young man Stephen; both were Jews from outside Jerusalem and Palestine. As we shall discover, Paul went on to become the spiritual leader of the Gentile Greek wing of the Church and came into conflict wit the Jersualem Jews because of his promotion of Gentile Christianity. But he was himself a Hellenistic Jew.

25 What was the form of the first Christian services?

Very few records are left to us upon the basis of which this question can be answered. It must be remembered, of course, that the first Christians were Jews and that they participated in the Temple and synagogue services as such. Their Christian services were *in addition to* their Jewish observances. They attended the regular services of their Jewish faith on the Sabbath (seventh) Day as all other devout Jews did. Then on the first day of the week they gathered together as groups of Christians inside the homes of their leaders and there discussed questions of special interest to them. They studied the Hebrew Scriptues, prayed, listened to men who demonstrated ability as teachers, and participated in some simple ceremonies which commemorated their Lord's death and resurrection.

26 What Scriptures did they study?

The only Scriptures in existence at the time were the Jewish books substantially as we have them in our Old Testament. They must also have read the books of the Apocrypha—not included in our Protestant Bibles—which were popular among the Jews of that day.

27 Were there no Christian writings?

None. The Christian Church was well launched on its career before any such were produced. There may have been private messages in written form which were passed from one congregation to another and read when the people came together to worship. But the New Testament contains no record of any such. The first Christian writing of which we have any knowledge was a letter written by Paul to the church at Thessalonica. There is still some debate as to whether First Thessalonians or Galatians is actually the older, but for our purposes it seems sufficient to accept the majority opinion which is in favor of First Thessalonians. But whichever may have been first, to Paul must go the credit for having written the first Christian book and for having launched the New Testament.

28 Was there no life of Christ in existence at that time?

There was current among the Christians and the Jews a considerable body of knowledge concerning Jesus, but no one had undertaken to commit it to writing in any formal way. As we shall see in a later study, there may have been some collections of the sayings of Jesus in written form, but they could have been nothing more than fragmentary notes. It is easy to assume that, because the four Gospels appear at the beginning of the New Testament, they are the oldest of the writings. But such is not the case; the New Testament began with Paul.

29 Did Paul set out to write a New Testament?

He did not. Nothing in any of his writings indicated that the need of a New Testament ever occurred to him. The only Scripture in which he was interested were those of the Old Testament. These were the ones he had in mind whenever he used the word "scripture." Whenever he studied the Scriptures, he studied the Old Testament; whenever he said the Scriptures were inspired, he referred to the Old Testament writings. He believed, of course, that some of his own words carried the endorsement of the Holy Spirit, and he expected them to be received as such (I Corinthians 2:4; 7:40; II Corinthians 5:5; I Thessalonians 4:8). But an open-minded reading of Paul's letters will make very plain the fact that he had no thought of writing scripture for us when he wrote his messages to the Christian churches for which he felt such a responsibility. Certainly he never referred to his own words, or to those of any other New Testament writer, as being scripture. There is a very great deal of difference between believing that one is writing scripture and believing that one is writing a message which has divine endorsement.

30 What is that difference?

Divinely inspired scripture, it is assumed, is designed to serve spiritual needs throughout all time. There is a quality of eternalness about spiritual truth which makes it useful in all generations. A man writing about a particular situation in a church might express truth which has an eternal meaning without attempting to do more than express a conviction concerning an immediate problem. He might write scripture without realizing he was doing so. This, apparently, is exactly what happened in the case of Paul. He was desperately concerned about certain spiritual and moral problems which arose within the Church and, under the guidance of the Spirit, wrote down the convictions of his soul and put them out with the confidence that they had divine endorsement. In doing so he actually produced scripture, for the things he said to the first-century churches are as true today when addressed to twentieth-century churches.

31 In what language did Paul write?

He attended the best Jewish schools and must have learned Hebrew and read the Old Testament in the original with ease. He was a Roman citizen and may have been familiar with Latin, though of that we cannot be sure. No doubt while attending school in Jerusalem he learned Aramaic, the common language of Palestine in that day. But he was a Greek by culture, and he preached in that language. The churches he founded were all in Gentile cities, and their congregations were made up of people who spoke Greek, for that was the universal language of the time. Very naturally, then, Paul wrote his letters to them in Greek.

32 When did Christianity break away from Judaism?

It is impossible to fix any precise date for such a break, for it was a process that went on through a period of years. During the first years of the Christian movement it was exclusively Jewish, though many members were Hellenistic Jews. A short time before Saul set out to persecute the Christians in Damascus, however, Philip had preached the gospel to the Samaritans (Acts 8:5) and had also baptized an Ethiopian officer. By A.D. 50 a very considerable number of Gentiles were included in the churches, but in each case the core of the group was Jewish. From about that time the scales began to dip in favor of the Greek wing of the Church, and in time the Jewish wing disappeared entirely. By A.D. 100 the Christian movement could very properly have been called a Gentile movement.

33 What part did Paul play in all this?

By birth, training, and experience, Paul was more cosmopolitan than the average leader of the Jerusalem Christians. They had had no contacts with the outside world except those provided by Jerusalem. It was natural, then, that he should begin thinking in world terms quite early in his Christian experience. His first missionary journey found him turning from the Jews to the Gentiles (Acts 13:46), and the chief item in his report to the church in Antioch of Syria was that God "had opened a door of faith to the Gentiles." This seems to have been the occasion for calling a council of the Church at Jerusalem (Acts 15), where Paul took an active part in securing exemption for the Gentiles from many of the Judaistic requirements.

There came a time when the Gentile world called to Paul in a dramatic fashion. He saw a man from Europe, in a dream, beckoning to him and pleading that he come to Europe and preach (Acts 16:9), and in obedience to that call he set out on a career that made him the great Apostle to the Gentiles and took him to every great metropolitan center of the empire. In time he became the foremost formulator of Christian doctrine and, next to Jesus himself, the most influential personality the world has ever known. As he fashioned the Church, he fashioned the world. The space limits of this study make it impossible to go into detail concerning the various activities and events of Paul's life. Our interest is primarily in his writings, and we will make only such historical inquiries as are directly related to them. After all, it is the purpose for which the New Testament books were written which will determine their values for us.

17

This is sometimes a very difficult problem. But if we can know something about the date of the writing of a book, the author, the persons to whom it is addressed, and the circumstances under which it was written, we will be greatly aided in our inquiry. Such questions are, after all, only the same questions we ask about any other literary composition. This means that, no matter what our opinion may be concerning the "inspiration" of the Scriptures, we must seek the truths that lie embedded in them as we seek the truth to be found in any other writing.

35 Are the Scriptures like any other writing, then?

No. But they must be read as other writings are read—with a mind open to receive whatever truths they contain. This means that they must be read with a religious mind, for they are religious writings. They were never intended as scientific textbooks, but as compositions expressing religious truths. An astronomer, for instance, reading the book of Psalms for information concerning the stars would probably feel his time had been wasted, even though there are references to the stars in the psalms. An economist reading the psalms for information concerning conditions in ancient Judah might glean a few facts which would be of interest to him. But since the psalms are, primarily, religious poems which express spiritual truths, they will yield their great treasures to the person who reads them for the purpose of discovering their spiritual value.

36 Did Paul write the first Christian book?

So far as we know, he was the first Christian ever to put Christian truth into written form; and according to the opinion of careful scholars, this occurred about A.D. 50.

37 What did he write?

He wrote a series of letters to Christian churches for the purpose of answering questions, settling controversies, outlining doctrines, stamping our heresies, restoring order, providing moral guidance, etc. Because every church had some interest in the letters received by other churches, these epistles of Paul's began to circulate among the congregations, and in time had a very great influence on the whole Christian movement.

38 To whom was the first letter written?

There is some small disagreement on this subject, but because the weight of opinion seems to favor the first letter to the Thessalonians, we will make a study of that book first.

39 Who were the Thessalonians?

A congregation of Christians in the city of Thessalonica (the modern city is called Salonika), a coastal town of northern Greece in a Roman province called Macedonia. Paul had organized them into a church in the course of his first journey into Europe.

40 How did this come about?

After some years of preaching in the region of Damascus, and missionary work in Galatia, Paul began to think of the Christian movement in world terms. About A.D. 48 or 49 he had his vision of a man from Macedonia calling for help, and as a result he set out for Europe. Sometimes traveling with another preacher, and sometimes traveling with only a companion, he worked his way across Macedonia and Greece, as he had through Asia, founding churches at great population centers. These, after a brief period of training and instruction, were left to themselves, but Paul continued to hold himself responsible for them and considered himself to be their spokesman on several occasions when a controversy was raging. They in turn looked to him for counsel and guidance. The word of no one else carried such authority among them. Occasionally a companion was sent out on a preaching mission, and in emergencies Paul wrote letters to his congregations. These letters are the earliest Christian documents we have, and are of the greatest historical value as well as of spiritual importance. They frequently throw much light on questions connected with the inner life of the first-century Church.

41 When did Paul organize the Thessalonian church?

Paul had had considerable experience as a preacher of the Christian gospel in the course of his missionary work in Galatia.

As a result of his preaching Gentiles had offered themselves for membership in the churches, and a general council of the Church was held in Jerusalem about A.D. 48 or 49, at which the whole question was discussed thoroughly and at great length. Paul seems to have been an active participant in that meeting, in spite of the fact that he was not one of the original eleven disciples. In the opinion of the people, the early followers of Jesus were the ones most competent to speak for the Church; but Paul seems to have stood up against them, asserting his right to speak because of the inner assurance he had from the Spirit of God.

At any rate Paul left that meeting in Jerusalem determined to carry the gospel to the Gentiles in an enlarged and intensified campaign. He went back over much of the same territory he had covered in the regions round about Damascus, Antioch, and Tarsus, and in the course of time found himself at the seaport of Troas, not far from the site of the ancient city of Troy. Here he had the vision of the Macedonian calling for help, and inspired by that experience he crossed over into Europe.

His first preaching was done at the city of Philippi, a Macedonian metropolis of great importance just a little way back from the seaport town of Neapolis, the point at which he landed on European soil. Here he founded a church which became in later years the most comforting congregation for Paul in all Christendom. He does not seem to have stayed long at Philippi, but soon pressed on to Thessalonica, where he remained for several months preaching. This was the political and commercial hub of Macedonia, and to it men and ships gravitated from all over the eastern end of the Mediterranean. It was probably in the spring of the year 49 or 50 that Paul began his ministry in Thessalonica—a work that continued through a number of months until perhaps late in the fall or even early in the winter.

42 What happened when he arrived in Thessalonica?

Throughout his entire life Paul remained a loyal Jew. In spite of animosity and persecutions he never failed to declare himself to be a good Jew of the strictest sect (Acts 22:3; 23:6; 26:5). It was perfectly natural then, that upon his arrival in Thessalonica he should ask for and find the local synagogue and make himself known to the leaders of the Jewish community. They received him with at least some sympathy, and for three successive Sabbaths he preached from their pulpit, explaining the Christian faith.

43 How did the Thessalonians receive him?

There were apparently two groups. (1) There may have been serious-minded Macedonians who had failed to find spiritual satisfaction in the current paganism in the midst of which they lived and had turned to the more exalted morality and chaste idealism of Judaism in the hope that they might find the satisfaction they had sought so earnestly. The Jews of that century were zealous missionaries of their faith, and wherever a synagogue was established a vigorous missionary campaign was in progress. The strict legalism imposed upon the converts was pretty arid, yet it was a distinct advance over the sensuality and spiritual poverty of the pagan religions which it was attempting to supplant.

(2) The second group were those individuals, to be found in every community, whose spirits were sensitive to spiritual appeals. Such are the God-fearers, without whom any nation or generation would be poverty stricken in the things of the soul. Just because the Greek learning had opened their minds, they turned wistfully toward any promise; but Judaism had not yet won them, for they were unable to submit themselves to the stern legalism which was of the very essence of Jewish religion. Whereas the first group had openly affiliated with the Jewish synagogue, the second group was frankly interested but remained aloof.

To both these groups the preaching of Paul made a great appeal. By the very nature of the case they were the sensitive spirits and responded to the exalted doctrines Paul preached. It would be expected that the Jews who had worked for long to make an impression on these people would be alarmed when they saw Paul making headway with their converts and prospects, and by the time the third Sabbath had passed they were ready to break openly with him. Thus the matter stood—the Jews were alienated, and the proselytes were interested.

44 What happened?

As was to be expected, the pious Jews were infuriated that a

21

stranger should walk off with their converts; and as Paul's success increased, they managed to start a riot for which Paul was blamed. As a consequence he was banned from the city by the Roman officials, and for the first time Christians were charged with disloyalty toward the empire.

45 What was the charge?

"They are all acting against the decrees of Caesar, saying that there is another king, Jesus" (Acts 17:7) was the wording of the charge. In other words, they were charged with sedition, and in the years that followed this charge was repeated many times, with frightful results. It was partly true, of course, for the Christians gave their supreme obligation and obedience to Jesus, their Lord; but that they were seditionists in the ordinary sense of the word was not true. Indeed, as the years went on, Paul made determined efforts to hold the Christians in line and dissuade them from taking violent action against the empire, no matter how serious the provocation might be (Romans 13:1-7).

46 Was this the end of the work in Thessalonica?

Paul was able to spend but a few months in Thessalonica, but in that time he gave the Christians such training as he could in the fundamentals of the faith. Inexperienced as they were, and without being stabilized in their Christian convictions, they were in danger of drifting back into paganism.

47 What did Paul do in the matter?

It was necessary to leave the church under such local and inexperienced leadership as was available, but Paul could not rid his mind of his anxiety for them. In addition to his fear that they might abandon their newfound faith, he also feared—and rightly—that they might suffer at the hands of the authorities because of their friendship for him. He had almost decided to return and face the music when he was taken with one of his periodic seizures of illness (II Corinthians 12:7; I Thessalonians 2:18). Unable to go in person, he sent Timothy, one of his assistants, to make inquiry as to the course of events and bring him the news. In the meantime he set out for Corinth with the expectation of spending some time in that city in missionary work.

48 What was Timothy's report?

Upon arriving in Thessalonica and making some investigation, Timothy was overjoyed to find that the Christian community was holding its ground, maintaining its loyalties, and prospering. Opposition continued, but the danger of defection seemed to be past. The news he could carry back to Paul would all be good.

When the news reached Paul, he was greatly heartened, and immediately sat down and wrote the Thessalonians a letter. This letter we have in the new Testament under the title "First Thessalonians."

49 What kind of a group were the Thessalonian Christians?

The Thessalonian church had been composed in considerable part of humble people without social prominence or influence. The members were working people whom Paul had met in the shops and market places (I Thessalonians 4:11), and who had suffered the miseries that go along with a financial depression. Some few of them were property owners, and another few were aristocratic women. When Paul had been compelled to leave the city, he had left behind him a congregation of people only half instructed, without a line of Christian writing, with no ritual or discipline, and with no record of the life and teachings of Jesus save that which he had given them by word of mouth. This was a very inadequate basis upon which to build a church.

50 What about the depression?

The city of Thessalonica was the center of the sail and tent business for the eastern Mediterranean, and many shops for the manufacture of this kind of equipment filled the waterfront. Sometime previous to Paul's arrival in the city the Roman government's reorganization of its agricultural program had resulted in the calling of real estate loans and the strangling of commerce. Ships lay idle in the harbors, and hundreds of skilled workers from the sailmaking trade tramped the streets in search of work. Paul was a tentmaker and depended upon his trade for his living as any other craftsman. He seems to have suffered much as a result of the depression, and except for the fact that the Philippian church forwarded him funds (Philippians 4:16) he might have faced a very serious situation. It is extremely interesting to note the fact that the first scriptures of the New Testament were written by a workingman, and that he wrote during a depression.

51 How had the Thessalonian church stood up?

No specific word from Timothy's report appears in the New Testament, and we can only infer what it contained. But we known that the Thessalonian church became in time one of the most vigorous and faithful in all the Christian movement. In the ninth century it sent two brothers as missionaries—Cyril and Methodius—who evangelized the Bohemians and Moravians. From this stock came John Huss, the forerunner of the Reformation, and Peter Boehler, a Moravian missionary to the Georgia Indians who was also the spiritual teacher of John Wesley.

52 What was the news about the Thessalonians?

That they had been faithful and loyal, and that they were anxious for the return of the missionaries. Persecutions were still going on, with the Jews as ringleaders, but also participated in by Gentiles. Some slanders concerning Paul had been spread, and some misunderstandings of his teachings were creating confusion. Several deaths had ocurred among the members, and this had raised a problem. Then, of course, there were some who had turned back to paganism.

53 What were the slanders concerning Paul?

It was said that he was immoral, mercenary, and conceited.

54 What about the misunderstandings of his teachings?

He had taught them to expect the early return of Jesus, and this had encouraged some to quit work while awaiting his return. This was so common that the Thessalonian church was getting a bad reputation.

55 What about the problem of the deaths?

Since some had died without seeing the Lord's return, there was a question as to what their fate might be.

The Jerusalem church had sent a written message to the Antioch congregation some years before Paul's visit to Thessalonica, but no word of it remains. It consisted of no more than a letter of credentials (Acts 15:23-29). Aside from this, Paul's letter to the Thessalonians was the first avowed piece of Christian writing ever to come into existence so far as we are able to discover.

Consider the vast number of tracts, books, and treatises that have poured into the libraries since that day, all dealing with some phase of the Christian religion. Think of the vast volume of reading matter the Christians have supplied the world. Then remember that it all started with Paul's letter to the Thessalonians. No other religion or movement has ever produced such a volume of literature as has Christianity, *and Paul started it!*

57 What did the letter contain?

First of all, Paul complimented the Thessalonians on the quality of their faith and assured them that the news of it had gone everywhere (1:2-10). He then proceeded to defend himself against the slanders that had been circulated concerning him (2:3-10). He is well aware of the price they have paid for changing their religion (2:14-15) and commends them for their steadfastness. But they are not the only ones who have suffered. He too has undergone a great strain in their behalf (2:17–3:10); and when his anxiety became too great, he sent them Timothy to strengthen and encourage them, and bring him news of their condition. With a message of deep affection he closes the first part of his letter (3:11-13).

Beginning with the fourth chapter, Paul launches out on a new line. The Thessalonian Christians are to undertake to develop their spiritual life (4:1 f.). Of course they have been doing this, but now they must invest more effort. Then comes a discussion of the problem of sex and marriage, with an appeal that this whole area of life shall be respected as something sacred (4:3-8)—something new to the pagan mind. Some of the people have quit work in anticipation of the return of Jesus (4:9-12), and others are worried about friends who have died without seeing Jesus (4:13-18). Paul orders the idle back to work and warns the others that they must be vigilant but composed in anticipation of the day of their Lord's return, so that they may not be unprepared (5:1-11). After a few words for the leaders of the church and some comments on the general nature of the Christian life (5:12-22), the letter closes with a benediction (5:23-28).

58 What happened when the letter arrived?

We must depend upon our imagination for the answer to this question. The church was probably called together, and then someone was appointed to read the communication to the assembled congregation. We can almost imagine the thrill that went through the little company. These humble people, with limited learning, have a letter from a great thinker whom they have known only as a fellow workman. No doubt it was read again and again, with every sentence and every word coming under the closest scrutiny. Some may have been irritated by occasional statements, but on the whole the congregation must have been greatly impressed. It would be perfectly natural for them to assign great authority to the letter, and every question that could be settled by reference to it was considered in the light of its teachings. As visiting Christians joined them in worship, it was read to them, and the news of its existence began to spread through the Christian world.

59 Did the letter settle their problems?

No more than it has settled all the problems of all the churches since. But it did give a substantial basis for settlement, though Paul's doctrine of the Second Coming did make trouble.

60 What about the second coming of Jesus?

The immature Thessalonians experienced two difficulties: (1) they developed extravagant and absurd ideas concerning the reappearance of Jesus, and (2) some members lapsed into ridiculous conduct because of the interpretation they put on the doctrine. News of this condition reached Paul, at work in Corinth, and it gave him no small anxiety. His concern was intensified by his sense of personal responsibility. He had founded the Thessalonian church, and its success or failure would go far toward determining the course of future missionary work. If it would be necessary to spend long years with a congregation, training and maturing the Christians, the work would go so slowly that any thought of world conquest would be out of the question. On the other hand, if it would be possible to set up a church after a few months of preaching, then cultivate it by correspondence, it might be possible for an evangelist like Paul to turn the world upside down. But this upheaval concerning the second coming of Jesus threatened the whole structure of the work.

61 What did Paul do?

He wrote the Thessalonians a second letter, which has been preserved for us in the New Testament and is called "Second Thessalonians."

62 When was it written?

It is impossible to fix the date exactly, though it could not have been more than a very few months after First Thessalonians was written. Certainly, the two letters were composed inside of a year, and both were written from the city of Corinth in Greece.

63 What was the great trouble in the Thessalonian church?

Some of the converts, believing that Jesus' second coming was very near, lived in a state of constant excitement. Many of them quit working entirely and lived off the charity of friends. The Christian services were rapidly developing into something not far removed from orgies. Then, to make matters worse, someone had forged Paul's name to a letter authorizing such conduct.

64 What was the cause of all this?

In the hands of these unschooled Christians the doctrine of the Second Coming had become a vagary. In the words of Dr. John H. Jowett, the great British preacher, Paul preached to the Thessalonians "not the cross of Christ but the coming of Christ." His doctrine had been perverted by the Thessalonians, and the church was in danger of being faced with an open scandal.

65 What did Paul really believe about the Second Coming?

He believed it was very near. He told his converts that their whole duty was to serve God and wait for the coming of his Son from heaven (I Thessalonians 1:9-10). He promised believers special favors which they were to receive on the day of their Lord's return (I Corinthians 1:7-8). He believed that when the last trumpet sounded and time had come to an end, then the faithful who were alive would be caught up into the air to meet their Lord and thereafter would be with him forever (I Thessalonians 4:16-17). There are other hints concerning his beliefs in at least two other New Testament books (Romans 2:16; 13:11; II Corinthians 5:10). The disciples taught this doctrine in some form at least, and Paul either got it from them or believed he had it as a special revelation. He firmly believed his own generation would witness the second coming of Jesus; but, later as his hopes were deferred and no sign of the approaching end appeared, he seems to have changed his mind somewhat. After his first three letters (I and II Thessalonians and I Corinthians) he gives the subject less and less attention, though he does say in later letters that Christ is to be the final judge (Romans 14:10; II Corinthians 5:10). But the bulk of his discussion is to be found in I Thessalonians 4:13-18 and II Thessalonians 2:1-12.

66 What can modern Christians believe about the matter?

Augustine said very frankly that he was puzzled by Paul's words. He did not know what the Apostle meant. Canon Farrar, the great English scholar, said, "So far as it is of doubtful meaning, it can have no value for us." Yet there is a very great interest in the doctrine, and devout people want to know what they can believe. Much of the confusion has resulted from the fact that we have been unwilling to admit that Paul was mistaken in any respect. But certainly Jesus did not return in Paul's time in the manner he evidently expected he would return. Any sane interpretation of the doctrine must begin with that simple fact.

Then we need to remember that the doctrine rests upon no recorded word of Jesus. In Acts 1:11 the angels at the Ascension are quoted as saying, "This Jesus, who was taken up from you into heaven, will come in the same way as you saw him go into heaven." On one occasion Jesus did say, "I will come again and will take you to myself" (John 14:3), but obviously he was not at that moment discussing any "second coming." If a belief in a second coming had been absolutely vital to Jesus' gospel, we can be sure he would have made that perfectly plain, as he did in the case of the necessity of repentance.

67 What facts can be wholly accepted?

1. The disciples expected an early return.
2. Paul expected an early return.
3. The Jerusalem church expected an early return.
4. The first-century Church expected an early return.

68 Is this all we know?

Certain other facts are self-evident, or they can be easily verified: (1) The return did not occur in Paul's day in the form he expected it. (2) Such a return has not yet occurred. (3) The failure of Jesus to return as expected created much difficulty for the early Christian Church. (4) Entire books or portions of books in the new Testament were written for the purpose of clearing up the thinking of the Christians on this subject. (5) Paul gave it less and less attention as his ministry progressed. (6) Many dates have been set for the return, but none has ever proved to be correct. (7) All efforts to figure out the time have thus far proved altogether fruitless, there being no better evidence in the case now than in the beginning. (8) Jesus disclaimed all knowledge of any date that had been fixed. (9) Controversy over the subject had divided the Church and embittered Christians toward one another. (10) Such a subject, then, should be dealt with very cautiously, lest greater harm than good result.

69 What can we conclude about the matter?

Certainly we can conclude that Paul was mistaken in thinking it would occur in his lifetime. Nineteen hundred years is too long to be called "an early time." Inasmuch as the doctrine is no part of Jesus' teachings, we can conclude that it was a part of the teachings of the original disciples. They could have come by the belief in any one of three ways: (1) on the basis of some word of Jesus which has not been preserved for us and of which we know nothing, or (2) by interpreting some word in the New Testament in a way we do not interpret it, or (3) they could have reasoned that he would have to return because he had not done the Messiah's work during the time of his first coming.

We may be sure that Jesus will ultimately triumph over all his foes, for the final victory belongs to him. He is alive and active in the affairs of men today, and is actually leading and guiding individuals in their attacks on sin and evil. No Christian who believes that Jesus is the Son of God would deny for a moment that he could come back in a second apparance, but it must be admitted that it has not happened in the way Paul and the first-century Church expected it to happen. Neither can it be established by the New Testament that any man can identify a date upon which such a reappearance may be confidently expected. Therefore we will be wise to fix our minds and plan our lives on the basis of at least three principles: (1) We have no right to make belief in some doctrine a test of Christian sincerity, denying Christian fellowship to those who do not accept our interpretation thereof, unless Jesus makes the matter prefectly plain. (2) No man who awaits Jesus' second coming dare wait in idleness, lest he bring reproach upon his Lord. (3) Belief in the doctrine is no warrant for withdrawing from participation in all efforts other men are making to work the will of God on earth as Jesus prayed (Matthew 6:10).

71 Under what circumstances was the second letter written?

Paul was still working and preaching in Corinth. Timothy and Silvanus, his friends, were with him. He was aware that the Thessalonians were still being persecuted and that they were making a brave stand, but the second letter was written for the purpose of instructing the Thessalonians on other matters, and in doing so Paul wrote one of his strangest epistles.

72 In what respect is it strange?

The resurrection of Jesus was the doctrine upon which Paul probably had his strongest convictions (I Corinthians 15:14), yet he makes no mention of this idea in either letter to the Thessalonians. Neither is the cross of Christ mentioned, though it is a favorite theme with the Apostle. He mentions the death of Jesus but once (I Thessalonians 2:15)—a remarkable fact—and even then it is given no theological significance. Nowhere in the letter does the word "law" appear, though obedience to the ceremonial requirements of Judaism was a burning issue in the Church. Though it is of small importance, it is interesting to note that Second Thessalonians is the shortest letter Paul ever wrote to a church on a great theme. In many ways the two Thessalonian letters are very similar.

73 In what respect are they similar?

First of all, they are alike in their plan. Each opens with a section on doctrine, and then about two-thirds of the way through a benediction appears (I 3:11-13; II 2:16-17), followed by a section of practical advice. In the second place, sayings of the first letter are duplicated in the second (I 2:9 is almost exactly like II 3:8), and in both letters there are numerous expressions of gratitude for the Thessalonians (I 1:2, 2:13; 3:9; and II 1:3; 2:13). Numerous references to Jesus' return are found in both (I 1:10; 3:13; 4:13-17; 5:27; and II 1:7-10; 2:1-12). In both letters the Christians seem to be suffering from persecution (I 2:14; II 1:4-6).

74 What was the occasion of the second letter?

Many Thessalonians conceived the idea that the advent of Jesus had ushered in a new era. They had welcomed the gospel Paul had preached (I 1:5-9), but in his absence the messianic hope had developed out of all proportions. In his first letter Paul had ventured a warning (I 4:11-12), but the situation had got out of hand. Plainly something had to be done or the Thessalonian church would set an example which would work grave injury on any plans Paul might have for spreading the faith through Europe.

75 How did the idea get started?

The doctrine of the Messiah was a very old one among the Jews. It taught that an age was coming when a divinely chosen leader would appear among the Jews to lead them through a political reorganization which would eventually result in a complete triumph for the nation with all its enemies destroyed and its rule established over all the earth. This doctrine, with some variations, had been taught by several Old Testament prophets, and had taken a great hold on the imagination of the people.

31

The Christians believed Jesus was that Messiah, but in believing so they had to alter the picture of the Messiah's kingdom somewhat to make room for the facts of Jesus' life and career. Certainly he had died without setting up any such political rule as the messianic hope usually called for. But the doctrine of the Second Coming suggested the possibility that, in his second appearance, he would announce his kingdom and his kingship, and all the earth would become subject to the Jews.

It is quite possible that Paul, in preaching to the Thessalonians, said something which encouraged them to believe this age had begun because Jesus had come to earth. At any rate, some members of the church got the idea and began fashioning their lives by it, becoming loafers and busybodies in the process.

76 Does this represent Paul's idea?

Not at all. His own life was one of industry and frugality, and he took great pride in the fact that he provided for his own expenses (I Corinthians 9:18). He did have a definite belief about the Messiah, however.

77 What was Paul's idea of the Messiah?

He believed Jesus was the Messiah and that, though he had not performed all the Messiah's work while on earth, he would come back and complete the assignment. He told the Thessalonians that the Messiah's day of judgment would come upon them like a thief in the night without warning (I 5:2), but in his second letter he modified that position somewhat and introduced another figure—the Antichrist.

78 What was the Antichrist?

Paul nowhere uses the word "antichrist" in any of his letters, the first use of the word occurring in First and Second John (I 2:18, 22; 4:3; and II 7), which are writings of a much later date. But he does make use of the idea without making use of the word. There was an old and popular belief current among the Jews to the effect that there was to be a prolonged conflict between good and evil which was to be climaxed by a terrific struggle between two creatures that would be the embodiment of two forces. Evil would be represented by one and goodness

32

by the other. Evil might be expected to grow more and more powerful, and more and more arrogant, until it seemed that the whole earth had been given over to it. But at the critical moment God's Christ would appear as the embodiment of goodness and overthrow all evil and its works.

79 How does Paul use the idea of the Antichrist?

In Second Thessalonians (chap. 2) he states this belief—as though he shared it—and calls attention to the fact that such an Antichrist has not yet appeared. Something is holding it back, and Paul believes that "something" is the Roman Empire. Thus he argues that the messianic age has not yet dawned because this conflict has not yet occurred. He is sure that Antichrist will make his appearance in due time (2:1-12), accompanied by signs and wonders, but Christ will also appear and conquer him. In the meantime he exhorts them to hold steady, do their duty, maintain their lives in righteousness, and be prepared for the day that is coming (2:13-17). Having developed this idea, he closes his letter with some practical advices.

80 What are his practical advices?

Everyone must assume responsibility for his own needs by earning his own bread (3:6-16). In this Paul and his associates have set an example (3:8), there never having been a charge against any of them. Of course those unfortunate enough to be in actual need are to be assisted, but all others must submit to the rule, "If any one will not work, let him not eat" (3:10).

81 What about the Roman Empire as the restraining influence?

We have an interesting question here. The author of the book of Revelation evidently believed the Roman Empire with all its brutality was the Antichrist, whereas Paul, the Roman citizen, suggests that it is the force that is holding the Antichrist in check (2:6-7).

82 How is this discrepancy explained?

Paul was a Roman citizen and held the empire in great respect. He is careful to plead with the Christians to treat officers with deference and obey the Roman laws (Romans

13:1-10). He thought of Rome as the force that maintained law and order throughout the world and made it a safe place in which the Church could grow and prosper. Generally speaking, at the time Paul's letters to the Thessalonians were written the Christians were getting along very well inside the empire. The author of Revelation, on the other hand, was a prisoner on Patmos and a victim of Roman ruthlessness. He had witnessed Christians suffering under Roman tortures and was all too familiar with the sternly repressive measures Caesar was applying to the Church. He could think of Rome in no other terms than those of the Antichrist.

83 What does all this mean?

It means that two great Christian thinkers were in direct disagreement even in the first century of the Christian Church's life. In reading the New Testament we must make room for such disagreements.

84 What effect did these letters have on other churches?

So far as we know, they had no immediate effect. The Thessalonians read them, studied them, showed them to guests who happened to visit their worship services, and of course treasured them. But there is nothing to indicate that the letters circulated among the other churches for many years. From any record in the New Testament we can conclude that the Thessalonian church was the only one disturbed by the doctrine of the Second Coming at this time.

85 Did Paul preach the doctrine nowhere else?

He probably preached it in some form to all his churches, but it is not mentioned in other letters with the exception of Second Corinthians and Romans. In the meantime we must turn to the next letter—Galatians.

86 What is the letter to the Galatians?

Unlike Paul's other letters, which are addressed to individual churches, Galatians is addressed to a group of churches, and was supposed to be read by all. In it the Apostle reaches one of his highest levels of Christian thinking. It is said that Martin Luther reached his conclusions which produced the Reformation as a result of reading this book.

87 Who were the Galatians?

At this point we meet one of the most difficult problems for the scholars who are trying to determine the background facts of the New Testament. There were two regions Paul could have meant by "Galatia."

88 What were the two Galatias?

In north central Asia Minor there was an area which had been called Galatia for three centuries because it was inhabited by Gauls from western Europe. In 25 B.C. the Romans had reorganized Asia Minor and added several territories in the south to form an enlarged province of Galatia. The problem is whether by "Galatians" Paul meant the descendants of the Gauls (the "North Galatian Theory") or the Greeks who were under the same administration (the "South Galatian Theory").

89 Why were there Gauls in Asia Minor?

In the fourth century B.C. there was a migration of Gauls from what is now France to the south and east. They reached Rome in 390 B.C. and a century later invaded Greece. In 230 B.C. they entered Asia Minor and settled in the mountainous region along the Black Sea. The Romans conquered them in 189 B.C. but let their own princes rule them till 25 B.C. The Gauls were a Celtic people, with quite different language and culture from their Greek neighbors. Some who urge the North Galatian Theory have suggested that the tensions of this heritage might explain Paul's converts' "so quickly deserting him who called you in the grace of Christ" (Galatians 1:6).

90 Did Paul found churches in North Galatia?

About this we have no exact information. Acts refers twice to Paul's traveling "through the region of Phrygia and Galatia" (16:6; 18:23), which seems to mean North Galatia. The first reference may fit with Paul's saying "it was because of a bodily ailment that I preached the gospel to you at first" (Galatians 4:13), if this is interpreted to mean he was stricken with a fever that changed his route and sent him to the North Galatian mountains to recuperate. On the other hand Acts says nothing about his spending any time in "Galatia" on this trip "through" it, and churches in North Galatian cities are never mentioned in either the New Testament or other early writings. By contrast Acts tells much about Paul's work in South Galatia.

91 What is the story of Paul in South Galatia?

The persecution following Stephen's martyrdom scattered Christian missionaries all up and down the eastern shore of the Mediterranean. Most of them sought out the Jewish communities, but in the great Syrian metropolis of Antioch some of them "spoke to the Greeks also" (Acts 11:19-20). When numbers of these Gentiles were converted, and word of it reached Jerusalem, Barnabas was sent to investigate. On seeing the results he joined in the evangelistic campaign himself and, needing more help, went to Tarsus for Paul, who had largely kept in retirement since his conversion. For a year the two worked in Antioch, until the prosperity of the church inspired the congregation to launch a foreign mission program, and choose Barnabas and Paul to lead it (Acts 13:1-3). They went first to the island of Cyprus to the west of Antioch (Acts 13:4-12), and then north to the mainland of Asia Minor, where they landed in South Galatia. Here they journeyed on foot from city to city into the interior and then back by the same route. In spite of serious persecutions they preached and organized churches in the cities of Antioch of Pisidia, Iconium, Lystra, and Derbe (Acts 13:13–14:25).

92 What is meant by Antioch of Pisidia?

Pisidia was one of the older provinces incorporated by the Romans in their province of Galatia, and it had to be named to distinguish this Antioch from the larger Antioch in Syria. Derbe and Lystra were in Lycaonia, another of the southern areas in the Roman province.

93 Was Paul's work here a success?

There are several indications that it was. It will be remembered that Paul sent a young man named Timothy back to Thessalonica to get news for him. This young man, who became one of Paul's most trusted lieutenants, was recruited at Lystra (Acts 16:1-3). He and Gaius of Derbe accompanied Paul on his final journey to Jerusalem, as part of a delegation evidently delivering an offering from the major Gentile churches (Acts 20:4). Because of these and other references to Paul's churches in the southern cities, over against the lack of references to northern cities, a majority of scholars accept the South Galatian Theory.

94 What does the letter tell us about the Galatians?

As already noted, it was addressed to people whom Paul had personally "called . . . in the grace of Christ" (1:6), and who on his first visit had been especially considerate of his illness (4:13-14). They knew and loved Paul like a father (4:15, 19), and had wholeheartedly accepted the gospel of faith he had preached to them (3:1-3; 5:7).

95 Were the Galatian churches composed of Gentiles?

They were, in the main, and in the fact lies the significance of the letter. It was Paul's custom to preach first in the Jewish synagogue when he came to a new city (Acts 13:14-43; 14:1; 17:1-4, 10; etc.), but thereafter as Gentiles became interested he took up the work with them. In the Galatian churches most of the members were these people converted directly from paganism (4:8). This lay behind Paul's writing them now.

96 Why did Paul write to the Galatians?

It is a rather long and involved story. News reached Paul that a great upheaval had occurred within the Galatian churches, which was disturbing the people very greatly, and he felt under a solemn obligation to write them a strong letter covering the whole case. In doing so he achieved three results: (1) He gave us the earliest piece of church history in the New Testament. (2) He gave us the gist of the gospel he preached to the Gentiles. (3) He wrote one of the greatest books in the New Testament, and what has been called "a charter of spiritual independence."

97 What was the nature of the upheaval?

In spite of all the evidence in favor of Paul, the Jerusalem church was never quite able to accept him as a Christian apostle on the same basis as the disciples. They had known him as a persecutor and perhaps had never been able to forgive him completely. At any rate, when he began preaching to the Gentiles, the suspicion grew that he was not entirely safe as a leader, and in an effort to get the matter cleared up Paul made a trip to Jerusalem to confer with two leaders there. The certification they gave him was sufficient, even though it was not enthusiastic (Galatians 1:18-24), and fourteen years later he made another trip to go over the matter again (2:1). This time he had it out. An agreement was reached by which the leading apostles recognized him as having equal authority with them, but they assigned him the responsibility of preaching to the Gentiles while they preached to the Jews. In spite of these conferences, and at least one visit to Antioch by Peter for the purpose of inspecting the work, this Jerusalem opposition continued. Some time, probably while he was away in Macedonia, preachers arrived in Galatia from Jerusalem and told the converts that they had been imperfectly instructed by Paul. The result was that they flocked to the meetings of the new teachers and accepted the new regulations they imposed. To counter this movement Paul wrote his letter to the Galatians in defense of his ministry and of their primitive faith. In this incident we have a very revealing bit of evidence.

98   What does it reveal?

The average Christian probably thinks that the first-century Church was a body of individuals who held one opinion, were loyal to one Lord, and who were united in one faith. The fact is, however, that the Church was split into a variety of factions, with a considerable number of beliefs bidding for acceptance. Something of this diversity of viewpoint will be pointed out in the studies that follow in this series. Certainly all was not sweetness and light in the early Church.

99   What about that bit of early church history?

The four Gospels, as we will learn, professed to set forth different aspects of the life of Christ, and in doing so presented some historical material. But all were written long after the events of which they wrote. The book of Acts was a determined effort on the part of an unusually able writer to set down facts concerning the early history of the Church. Except for some of the later events in which Luke was a participant, this record is fashioned out of reports supplied the writer by other people.

38

But in the first two chapters of Galatians we have a bit of history out of the early life of the Church written by one who had participated in the events of which he was writing. As such these chapters constitute the earliest bit of church history we have in the New Testament coming from eyewitnesses. It is firsthand evidence. It has been called the "bedrock of early Christian history."

100 What does the history involve?

It is a report, all too sketchy of course, of those early years when the whole future course and character of Christianity was being decided. They were strenuous years, marked by sharp differences of opinion, by violent wrenchings of heart, by sharp cleavages, by heroic efforts to change a mental outlook, by vigorous debate, and by not a little hard feeling.

101 What was the issue at stake in Galatians?

For at least four hundred years, since the day of Ezra the Scribe, when the Law had been proclaimed and officially accepted as the divinely inspired constitution and way of faith for the Jews, they had gone on in the belief that they were in possession of the one sure way of salvation. In this they believed they were favored above all other people. They believed in a God who ruled all the earth, but they also believed they were the only people who knew how to win his approval. To enter upon this way and share in its benefits every non-Jew had to undergo certain rites and ceremonies, by which he was assured that he had become a Jew, spiritually speaking. There was, they believed, absolutely no other way of making sure of God's approval. The gate through which any Gentile must pass was narrow, exacting, and altogether inelastic. Once a Gentile had been admitted to the spiritual fellowship of the Jews, he was still under the necessity of observing Jewish law down to the most minute detail exactly as was expected of every other devout Jew.

102 Why this insistence that they become Jews?

According to Jewish belief, a promise had been made to Abraham, by Jehovah, to the effect that his seed should rule the earth. No man could share in the ultimate triumph of the Jews unless he was a Jew. This did not mean that only those with a Jewish blood stream could inherit the promises, for just what "Jewish blood" meant was a little uncertain, the blood of all the East being so mixed. But the Jewish law provided a process by which a non-Jew could become a Jew—so far as his spiritual identity was concerned—by undergoing certain rites and ceremonies. Because of this provision the Jews had a right to claim a certain liberalism.

103 Were the Jews out to convert Gentiles?

Confident that they possessed the only true knowledge of God, and believing they were destined by the promises made to Abraham to rule the world, the Jews of Jesus' time were conducting a vigorous campaign throughout the empire. With all this the Jerusalem church, for the most part, probably agreed. They thought of the Christian movement as something that must grow up inside Judaism, and not as something that could be preached independently of Judaism. They apparently never dreamed that Christianity would someday become a world religion, numbering adherents from all races and peoples. They supposed Jesus intended only to enrich Judaism, never thinking that he would supersede it. In their opinion it was absolutely necessary for any Gentile convert to become first of all a Jew, and after that a Christian.

104 What was Paul's position?

He believed that Jesus was superior to Judaism and that a person might become a Christian without becoming a Jew at all. In preaching Christ to the Gentiles he did not require them to undergo the rites required of one who was to become a Jew, nor did he subject his converts to the interminable list of regulations they would have been called upon to obey if they had been entering the spiritual fellowship of the Jews.

105 How important was the difference?

It made all the difference in the world. If the Jews were right, then Jesus had died in vain. He had not liberated people from anything. He had only added something to their spiritual burden; he offered them nothing beyond that which was already found in Judaism. If, on the other hand, Paul was right, then all the labored ritualism and elaborate ceremony of the Jews was outmoded. Jesus' death cleared the way so that any one could approach God and be assured of the forgiveness of sin on the basis of faith in Christ. The Law, with its infinite variations and ramifications, could be discarded. In a word, Paul proposed that the Gentile should by-pass Judaism and arrive at fellowship with God entirely on the basis of faith in Christ.

106 Did the Jerusalem Christians insist upon keeping the Law?

A considerable faction of the Jerusalem Church so insisted. The disciples seem to have conceded some points (Galatians 2), but some of the others were not able to achieve such spiritual liberality. This was the faction that sent preachers up to Galatia to preach the necessity of the Law to the Gentile converts. They even went as far as Corinth, disturbing Paul's converts in that city. Very clearly the controversy represented a crisis in the Christian movement.

107 Were those Jerusalem Christians mere bigots?

They may seem to be after the passage of all these centuries, but we must think of them very sympathetically. They had come into their faith the hard way, enduring hardships, persecutions, exile, and martyrdom. The Law to which they gave such slavish reverence was the product of the most devout scholarship of their race through hundred of years. Then, too, their faith was infinitely removed from the supersition that passes as religion among other peoples. Any Gentile who abandoned paganism and accepted the Jewish faith took a long step forward in religious thought and practice, and the Jews who went preaching the Law to the Gentiles were honest and sincere people who genuinely believed they were opening a door of privilege. With all this in mind it is easy to understand the way Paul shocked the Christian Jews with his doctrine of salvation by faith alone.

108 How did Paul shock them?

He told the Gentiles in effect that they did not need to become Jews at all; they only needed to accept Jesus as the Son of God who had opened the way to God; and that anyone could be assured of all the benefits of keeping the Law, and more, by believing on Christ and trusting God to do what Jesus had promised on God's behalf.

109 Had the Galatians believed Paul?

They had. His gospel had made a great appeal to them, and they had flocked to the Christian churches in a happy spiritual experience of forgiveness. This made them easy prey for the preachers from Jerusalem.

110 Who were those Jerusalem preachers?

No names have been preserved in the New Testament, but they were representatives of the extremist party who insisted upon the strict letter of the Law. They correspond to the extremists of today who refuse Christian fellowship to all those who do not accept their doctrinal interpretations of the Scriptures. The Jerusalem church seems to have been divided over the issue itself.

111 What was their mission in Galatia?

They arrived in Galatia with all the prestige of the Jerusalem church behind them and with letters of introduction from some of the disciples. Very naturally the half-instructed Galatians accepted them as being men of superior knowledge and listened to them with great respect. When these Jerusalem preachers, therefore, told the Galatians, in Paul's absence, that he was not really an apostle, never having seen Jesus in the flesh, it shook their faith and gave them a terrible sense of insecurity. When this was followed by the assertion that they must undergo the ceremonial rites prescribed by the Law, they offered themselves for the ceremonies without argument.

112 How successful were the Jerusalem preachers?

They seem to have carried the Galatian Christians with them. Everywhere the confused converts turned to Judaism. They should not be judged too harshly, for after all these new teachers had come from Jerusalem, the fountainhead of the movement, and their words inspired confidence for that reason. The poor Galatians had no rule by which to judge the matter.

They had set out to be Christians, and they wanted to be good Christians. The Jerusalem preachers were unquestionably sincere. They were Christians, and they came with a warning that the Galatians had been imperfectly instructed. Besides, they had the Scriptures to support them. He would be a brave Galatian indeed who would have ventured to object. The result was a complete disruption of Paul's work.

113 What did Paul do about it?

He wrote a letter to the Galatians under a very great stress of emotion. It was plain to him that the whole mission to the Gentile world was at stake. If he could not prove his case to them, he might as well abandon his program of carrying the gospel to the world. All this accounts for two peculiarities of the letter.

114 What are those two peculiarities?

First, he opens his letter in an unusual manner. Paul regularly begins with a carefully worded formal salutation. This is no mere conventionality; rather it is designed to remind his readers of the basis for his authority and pave the way for his message. In all the other letters the salutation is phrased with delicate finesse. But here Paul declares his apostleship bluntly and even belligerently.

In the second place, he closes his letter unusually. In all other instances he dictated to a professional letter writer who produced a manuscript that was a model of neatness. In this case he may have dictated the body of the epistle and then at the end (6:11) taken the pen from the scribe and in a big bold hand written the closing words (6:11-18) with something of the daring that characterized John Hancock when he signed the Declaration of Independence. It was the custom of the times to issue public proclamations in large letters and post them on some bulletin board where all the world might read. As one reads the letter to the Galatians one can easily imagine Paul under a passion of conviction writing those last words in poster style that they might be plainly understood. There is something of the spirit of Martin Luther about him. On the principles of faith which he has outlined he is willing to stand until death!

115 How did he proceed with his argument?

There was a second issue involved. The Jerusalem preachers had questioned his scholarship, his apostleship, and his message. With his first words he attacked this question.

116 What was his answer?

He opened his letter, as has been said, with a blunt assertion of his apostleship: "Paul an apostle—not from men nor through man, but through Jesus Christ and God the Father, who raised him from the dead" (1:1).

117 What did that mean?

After vigorously rebuking those who had doubted his right to speak as an apostle (1:6-9), he proceeded to justify his apostleship. In the most solemn language he declared that he had received his call to preach directly from Christ himself (1:12) and not from any human sources. In swift-moving passages he reviewed his personal religious experience, in which he had dealt directly with God (1:13-16), and as a result of which he had turned from being a persecutor to being an apostle. Without any commission from the disciples (1:17) he had proceeded to preach, and for three years had continued as an evangelist. Then, as if conceding something to the authorities, he had gone down to Jerusalem and conferred with Peter through a period of some fifteen days (1:18), at which time he had also had some conversation with James, the Lord's brother (1:19). Aside from this brief contact he had not been in any way dependent upon the Jerusalem leaders, though they took some pride in his work (1:24). Fourteen years later he had made another trip to Jerusalem and this time laid before the disciples the whole story of his mission to the Gentiles (2:1-2). This visit was rather for the purpose of reporting than for the purpose of securing credentials. But when the disciples had been fully informed as to what he was doing, they granted him the status of an apostle of equal authority with them (2:9). Thus Paul concludes that he has both divine and human authority for his work. His case is clear. He has as good a right to preach as anyone. He will concede to no one a superior right or authority.

44

118 Had that authority been questioned by the disciples?

Paul pointed with some pride to the fact that not only had the disciples never thereafter questioned his authority, but he had on at least one occasion taken issue with Peter himself—to whom he refers by the name of Cephas—rebuking that disciple for imposing Hebrew regulations on Gentile Christians without due warrant (2:11-14), and carried his point, thus further establishing his right to be heard as an apostle.

119 In what respect did he defend his gospel?

Paul was amazed that the Galatians, having once experienced the spiritual freedom of the gospel he had preached to them, should turn back to the cold legalism of the Jews. In an especially vehement passage (1:6-9) he denounced the Jerusalem preachers, even declaring that if an angel from heaven should preach their doctrines he would still insist they were false. Then, having defended his authority as an apostle (1:10-2:14), he proceeded to show that the only way anyone—Jew or Gentile—had ever found Christian salvation was through faith, never through the Law (2:15-21).

120 What did Paul mean by faith?

In the old days when Paul had been a persecutor of the Christians, no man had excelled him as a keeper of the Law. He was the strictest of the strict, but on the Damascus way he had met a new spiritual challenge, and in the days that followed he had accepted it, dedicating all his powers to the new way. This had resulted in a profound spiritual experience which produced a sense of spiritual relief, a consciousness of sins forgiven, and an inner conviction that the living Christ dwelt in him. This he called "faith," and in comparison with it the deadly formalism of Judaism was as nothing. Such an experience the Galatians had had (3:1-6), and now they were turning from the mountains to the valleys. This was what amazed Paul so greatly.

121 Did the Jerusalem preachers have no such faith?

They professed to have had a great spiritual experience, claiming to base their confidence on the fact that they were

Abraham's children. They believed that Jesus was the promised Messiah of the Jews, but they did not seem to think of him as the world's Savior—only the Savior of the Jews and such others as were willing to become Jews. Paul reminded them that it was Abraham's faith which had given him standing with God (3:7-9) and that only those who had faith could be called his descendants. The Jewish Scriptures had promises that the heathen should be blessed when they had such faith as Abraham had. Did this not prove the case? The fact that faith had worked in him was evidence that Paul was correct in his belief.

122 What did Paul believe about the Law?

He believed that it was a temporary expedient, ordained of God, intended to serve only until God should reveal himself through Jesus Christ (3:15-18). The Law, he said, was like the family servant in the ancient world who escorted the boy to school but turned him over to the schoolmaster at the door. So the Law had escorted the Jews through the centuries but must now turn them over to Christ (3:19-25). If anyone really believes in Christ, that person is the spiritual heir of all the promises made to Abraham, regardless of Jewish law (3:26-29). So also the day has come when the Christians, like the nobleman's son, have come of age spiritually, and as free people they call their God Father (4:1-7).

123 What was Paul's personal attitude toward the Galatians?

The easy way in which they had allowed the Jerusalemites to turn them aside from a liberal religion discouraged him terribly. He wondered if his efforts in their behalf had not been wasted (4:8-11). And yet they were very dear to him, and he could not give them up. With a passionate earnestness he pleaded with them to hold fast to his doctrines (4:12-5:12). He was well aware of the hazards involved, but assured them that the reality of their faith would be attested by fruits of the Spirit (5:13-24). If a man has these, he need not fear for the orthodoxy of his opinions or the accuracy of his theology. No one can have love, joy, peace, patience, kindness, goodness, faithfulness, gentleness, and self-control without the Spirit of Christ. Then with strong moral counsel he closed his letter (5:25-6:10).

124   What about the handwritten paragraph at the end?

It is a repetition of the central theme of the letter. In Philippi he had been beaten and still carried the scars—the brand of a slave. To these he points with pride, declaring himself a slave of Christ and challenging the Jerusalem preachers to show better credentials for their right to preach Christ (6:11-18).

125   How did Paul propose his letter should be used?

He sent it by a messenger to one of the churches, expecting it to be read to the assembled congregation and then forwarded to another, and then another, until its contents were known by all. It would seem reasonable to believe that the various congregations made copies to be consulted and studied at leisure. As visitors dropped in on the congregations, and heard the letter read, or were allowed to peruse it in their spare time, the fame of the epistle spread abroad, and in time it became one of the most treasured writings of the Christian Church.

126   What effect did the letter have?

Of that we have no record, but at least there is no word in the New Testament of further trouble among the Galatian churches. The Jerusalem preachers probably withdrew and left the field to Paul, whereupon the excitement subsided. During the next century, however, the Galatian churches became a hotbed of heresy in various forms, and one ancient Christian writer declared it was a land of sects and cults. Perhaps the volatile nature which was displayed by Paul's converts in being so easily swept off their feet by the teachers from Jerusalem was inherited by their grandchildren.

127   What is the modern value of the book?

Martin Luther held the Epistle to the Galatians in very high esteem, saying "The Epistle to the Galatians is my epistle. I have betrothed myself to it. It is my wife." Another writer has said, "It has done more than any other book in the New Testament for the emancipatioo of Christianity, not only from the yoke of Judaism, but from every other form of externalism that has ever threatened the freedom and spirituality of the gospel." Another has said, "The Church can hardly reckon how much she owes to such a writing." Ramsay, the great Scotch scholar, said, "It is a unique and marvelous letter which embraces in its six short chapters such a variety of vehement and intense emotion as could probably not be paralleled in any other work." Canon Farrar, the famous British scholar, said, "The words scrawled on those few sheets of paper were destined to wake echoes which have lived and shall live forever. . . . They are the Magna Charta of spiritual emancipation."

128 What letter did Paul write next?

He seems to have written his first letter to the Corinthians to the Christians in the city of Corinth. They made up one of the most important congregations, and to them Paul wrote at least four letters—more than he is known to have written to any other church.

129 Did Paul found the Corinthian church?

When his ministry ended so precipitately and disastrously in Thessalonica, he turned south with Timothy and Silvanus to Athens. From there he sent Timothy back to get a report, and passed on west to Corinth, where he began a preaching mission that continued through about eighteen months (Acts 18:11). During the time he was successful in establishing a strong Christian church, and from there he wrote his two letters to the Thessalonians.

130 What kind of city was Corinth?

It was the second city of Greece, yielding first place only to Athens. A great metropolis had stood on its site from ancient days, but in the year 146 B.C. the Romans destroyed it, and for one hundred years it lay in ruins. In the year 46 B.C., however, Julius Caesar caused it to be rebuilt, and it developed into one of the great cities of the eastern Mediterranean. Its location was highly advantageous, on the isthmus that connected northern with southern Greece. This isthmus is only about five miles wide, and all commerce between north and south had to cross over it. Moreover, the city could not be more than two or three miles from the sea on either side; and in Paul's day it was the custom to pull ships up on shore, slip great rollers under them, and haul them across the isthmus in order to save the trip around the peninsula by sea. All this meant that the city was the crossroad of the sea-lanes of the East. Trade could come up from either side and traffic with merchants from the ends of the earth. The whole condition conspired to make it inevitable that a city should grow up on the site. In Paul's day Corinth had a population of a quarter of a million freemen and twice as many slaves. But in addition to its commercial importance the city of Corinth was credited with being the most immoral city of the ancient world.

131 Was there any good reason for this condition?

First of all, it was a seaport with sailors from all parts of the Mediterranean treading its streets and frequenting its temples and amusement places. Any cosmopolitan center which thrives on foreign trade becomes immoral as it undertakes to pander to the tastes of visitors who have left all moral scruples at home. Business would raise no restraints which would interfere in any way with trade. In Paul's time the immorality of the city was proverbial throughout the world, and to "corinthianize" meant to play the harlot. The Temple of Venus, one of the most magnificent structures in the city, housed one thousand prostitutes whose business it was to serve the strangers who visited the city.

132 What kind of religion did Corinth have?

There was prevalent at the time a type known to modern scholars as "mystery religions." It gave much emphasis to religious meals, rites, ceremonies of initiation, and a certain mystical communion with divinities whom the Corinthians called "Lord" and "Savior." But for the most part religious life was at a very low ebb in Corinth, and the old Greek gods were burlesqued on the stages of local theatres for the amusement of blasphemous crowds. Nowhere in all the city was there any force, religious or social, which imposed any moral restraints upon the native inhabitants or their visitors.

133 Was this not a difficult city in which to launch a mission?

This was precisely the problem Paul faced, and as he came down to Corinth from a humiliating experience in Athens (Acts 17:16-34), he was in none too confident a state of mind. The Corinthians prided themselves that they were superior to

Athens in literary, philosophical, and intellectual matters; and this superior attitude, combined with a rampant immorality, made the city the most difficult in all the world in which to launch an ethical religion.

134 Did Paul realize all this?

He was fully aware of it. He knew he was not an eloquent preacher, gifted with the graces of an actor, or capable of weaving an oratorical spell over a crowd. His experience in Athens had taught him that he must make an altogether different approach. He was sure that he was not capable of making a dramatic impression on the sophisticated Corinthians (II 10:10; 11:6), and so he approached the city with fear and trembling (I 2:3; Acts 18:9).

135 How did he open his campaign?

This seems to have been a problem to him. His attack on the idolatry of Athens had been much less than successful. To open a direct assault on the immorality of Corinth by appealing to a nonexistent conscience was to invite failure from the start. If he undertook to appeal to the sophisticated learning of Corinth, presenting Jesus as a new problem in ethics, philosophy, or metaphysics, this was likewise to invite disaster, for he was no forensic match for the rhetoricians and orators who crowded Corinth's lecture halls and discoursed for fat fees.

136 What did they have to do with it?

Corinth, like any other Greek or Roman metropolis, was inundated at all times by a flood of teachers and lecturers who professed to teach some new "principle" of life. They were somewhat like the modern "psychologist" who rents the ballroom of a swanky hotel and lectures at extravagant fees to fashionable women. These ancient orators were usually skilled in the arts and tricks of public speech and preached promising doctrines not entirely unlike those of certain pseudo psychologists who appeal to the self-styled intelligentsia of modern times. They were stylish, brilliant, clever and entertaining. In competition with all such Paul was at a great disadvantage. First of all, he was not a brilliant speaker. Then he seems to have been of unpromising personal appearance. He earned his living at his trade of tentmaking as he went, and could not have presented a stylish appearance. Finally, the doctrine he proposed called for a strict and rigid discipline which did not commend itself to a dilettante world. The doctrine of the resurrection of Jesus had to compete with the sensuous teachings of the lecture halls and mystery religions.

137 What did Paul decide to do?

He finally determined to present to the Corinthians just one message—Jesus Christ, and him crucified (I 2:2; 3:10 f.). He determined to strike directly at the basic structure of paganism—not seeking merely a reformation, but a complete replacement of life. He would challenge the wickedness of the city without any attempt at cleverness or subtlety. In Thessalonica he had preached on the theme of the true God with emphasis upon the coming of his Son, and his second coming, to save the people from the day of wrath (I Thessalonians 1:9 f.); but in Corinth he would declare that Christ died for all people and that to believe in him would mean a resurrection of a new spirit on the part of the believer. To deal with the immortality of the city he had to place over against it a type of life that would contrast sharply; he had to deny the power of anything else to amend matters in the least (I Corinthians 1:9, 30; 2:12 ff.; 6:11, 14 ff.; 10:16; 12:3; 15:1).

138 Was this something new?

Probably not. It is altogether likely that he had preached along this same line many times. He believed that the Spirit of Christ entering a man's spirit made a new creature out of him. This was his basic belief, and everything else in doctrine was to be judged by that. When he condemned idolatry, it was because he believed it made union with Christ impossible (I 10:14). When he warned against licentiousness, it was because he believed the Christians were married to the Lord Christ (I 6:15). This identity between the believer and Christ was the controlling principle in the new faith.

139 What success did Paul have in Corinth?

He seems to have won a considerable number of people of all classes (I 1:26; 7:21), but his special success was in converting

51

some of the more prominent citizens. The fact that he mentions persons by name in his letter (I 1:11-16; 16:15-17) suggests that they enjoyed some social status, and the importance of two of them is attested by references to them elsewhere in the New Testament (Acts 18:8; Romans 16:23).

140 Were they all Gentiles?

In the book of Acts we have the names of certain Jews at Corinth who became Christians—Aquila, Priscilla, and Crispus—and Paul himself hints that there were open-minded Jews there (I 1:2, 24; 12:13). However, the others he names—Chloe, Gaius, Fortunatus, Achaicus, and Stephanas, who seems to have been the leading layman of the church—were presumably Greeks.

141 Did Paul have any trouble with the Jews in Corinth?

It will be remembered that the two letters to the Thessalonians were written from Corinth, sometime during Paul's eighteen-month stay in that city; and there are those who profess to believe there is a hint in his first letter (I Thessalonians 2:15; 3:7) that he was in trouble with the Jews in Corinth as he had been in trouble with them in Thessalonica. Acts 18:12 supports this belief. An effort was made to prod the Roman proconsul into acting against Paul; but that officer, being a learned man, and knowing something of the character of the people with whom he was dealing, refused, so that Paul labored on without official interference.

142 What was the final result?

It is no small testimony to the effectiveness with which Paul preached, and the sagacity with which he planned, that at the end of eighteen months a thriving church had come into existence in Corinth. Though it was far from perfect, and though it was made up of people with very little experience in the Christian way, a definite start had been made (Acts 18:1-17). When Paul was satisfied that the new organization could stand alone, he departed for Ephesus, which was only two days' sailing to the east; and after a brief period of preaching in Ephesus (Acts 18:19-21), he departed for Jerusalem to attend a feast. This was followed by an evangelistic tour of Galatia and

Phrygia (Acts 18:23), which finally brought him back to Ephesus (Acts 19:1).

143 What happened at Ephesus?

Paul's preaching seems to have been attended by remarkable results, for Acts records that "all the residents of Asia heard the word of the Lord, both Jews and Greeks" (19:10). Our immediate interest in his stay in Ephesus, however, arises from the fact that it was from that city that Paul wrote his letters to the church at Corinth.

144 How did he happen to do this?

Inasmuch as Corinth and Ephesus were not far removed from one another (two days' sailing), it was quite natural that there should be considerable travel between them. Among those who made a trip from Corinth to Ephesus were some unknowns to whom Paul refers as being "Chloe's people" (I Corinthians 1:11). From these travelers Paul got bad news concerning the church in Corinth, as a result of which he wrote what we have in the New Testament under the name of "First Corinthians."

145 Who were these "Chloe's people"?

We have no way of knowing, precisely. It seems probable that Chloe was a member of the church in Corinth, and that these travelers were some of her household, perhaps servants or employees. They may even have been members of the family. They may or may not have been Christians, though if Chloe herself was a Christian and they were her servants, it is likely that they were also Christians. All we know, however, is that they reported to Paul a disgraceful situation which had arisen inside the church at Corinth.

146 What was that disgraceful condition?

There seem to have been several aspects of it: (1) The members were breaking up into petty factions. (2) The church had become critical of Paul himself. (3) Gross immorality had developed among them. (4) The observance of the Lord's Supper had become an open scandal.

147 What about the factions?

We know that the Church was plagued with numerous

controversies and that it had not yet reached a unanimous opinion concerning the exact nature of Jesus. Many teachers and preachers had many ideas, some of which differed widely. There was, as yet, no uniformity of doctrine or belief. Shortly after Paul left Corinth there appeared among the Jews at Ephesus a brilliant preacher from Alexandria by the name of Apollos. We have only scant records concerning this remarkable man, but he seems to have been an individual who possessed rare gifts and graces. He was learned in the Hebrew Scriptures and was apparently well trained as a religious teacher, but he knew little about Jesus, being a disciple of John the Baptist (Acts 18:24-25). Meanwhile Aquila and his wife Priscilla, the leading Jewish members of the Corinthian church, had come to Ephesus with Paul and stayed to work there. Hearing Apollos speak in the synagogue, they recognized his potentialities and undertook to win him over and give him a thorough theological education. When they graduated him, he chose to go to Corinth, where his eloquence in preaching and in debate seems to have made him quite a sensation (Acts 18:26-28). Some of the Corinthian Christians—perhaps his converts—were dazzled by his brilliance and announced themselves as his disciples, separating themselves from the rest of the church. This gave rise to disputes and disgraceful divisions among the Christians. There was no moral or religious difference between the factions—only a petty quarrel over the matter of leaders. The total result was a splitting of the church and the creation of a situation which Paul could not ignore.

148 How many factions were there?

At least four: (1) those who remained loyal to Paul, (2) those who followed after Apollos, (3) those who declared for Peter, and (4) a group who professed to receive messages and divisions directly from Jesus himself.

149 What fault did they find with Paul?

The Greeks set high store by any man who was gifted in the arts of public speaking and attention has already been called to the fact that Paul was not such a one. It is doubtful if any people have ever been more fascinated by those who could make an effective public address. As has already been said, orators swarmed over every great city ready to discuss the most profound or the most trivial subjects on a moment's notice, for a fee. For the most part they were highly gifted men, and in contrast with them Paul knew he had made none too good a showing. Especially did he show up to poor advantage in comparison with the silver-tongued Apollos (I Corinthians 1:12; 3:4; 4:6), as he himself freely admitted. This awkwardness on his part had become a matter of comment among the sophisticated Corinthians, who were not hesitant about discussing the matter to Paul's disadvantage. They wanted him to imitate the grandiose style of the professional lecturers who were so popular with the people, and his crude and forthright manner of speaking was being urged against him and weakening his influence with the church.

150 What about the immorality of the church?

Because of conditions already described, there was a large floating population in Corinth at all times. Ships from two seas put in at the city's harbors, and sailors were always crowding its streets on shore leave. With wages to spend and time to kill, they lived with abandon. Plenty of people were ready to help them get rid of their money. Ancient Corinth resembled some Oriental seaports of our day. Life was dissolute, and the popularity of the city's immorality was fostered and sanctioned by the dominant religion, with its temple to the goddess of love, who was also the patron of the city. Temple prostitutes presented lascivious dances as a part of public festivals and religious celebrations. Unnatural vices were practiced without rebuke or shame (I Corinthians 6:9-10). The vast majority of the city's population were slaves—unscrupulous, vicious, and brutalized. Exploited as they were, they involved their masters in their ruin. Altogether the city was a seething mass of corruption, and all this was seeping back into the lives of the Christians who, under Paul's ministry, had made such a brave beginning in the new "way." A particularly flagrant case was that of a man, a member of the church, who was living with his stepmother in open adultery. She was his father's widow, and the two were probably maintaining a common-law relationship; but it was a serious crime in the eyes of either the Roman or the Hebrew law. Yet the Corinthian church was condoning it.

151 What about the observance of the Lord's Supper?

It was the Christian custom for each individual, or family, to bring his own meat and drink to the Communion table. In time considerable quantities of such supplies were brought in for these occasions, for we must remember that at first the Communion supper was a real meal. Among the Corinthians it developed into an occasion of conviviality, with many Christians slipping into actual drunkenness. From that point on it was but a short step to the point where the holy festival was little less than an orgy. All this became known to Paul, and just at that moment an opportunity presented itself whereby he was able to do something about it.

152 What was that opportunity?

Three members of the Christian church suddenly appeared one day at the sail shop in Ephesus where Paul was employed, bringing with them a letter from the Corinthians which Paul was expected to answer. They were Stephanas, the leader of the Corinthian church, Achaicus, and Fortunatus (I Corinthians 16:15-18).

153 What did the letter contain?

This letter would be extremely interesting if we could but have a copy of it. Unfortunately it has passed out of existence, so far as we know, but it holds a very deep interest for us for the reason that, though Paul was himself a great letter writer, this is the only letter we have any record of his ever having received. What its contents must have been can only be guessed from the contents of his reply. It seems to have been composed in large part of questions, stimulated perhaps by his earlier letter.

154 Is this not Paul's first letter to the Corinthians?

In replying to this communication from the Corinthian church Paul speaks of having written to them before (5:9), from which it can be inferred that we have in the New Testament as First Corinthians is, actually, the second letter he wrote to the church at Corinth.

155 What became of the earlier letter?

We do not know, unless some part of it is contained in Second Corinthians 6:14—7:1.

What reason is there for such a belief?

Paul says that he had written them charging them to have nothing to do with immoral persons, even though these immoral folk may have called themselves Christians. If that was the only subject with which the letter dealt, it was probably a brief epistle. The section of Second Corinthians which is sometimes said to be the "lost letter" is quite detached from the rest of the book in its present setting and could very easily have been the first letter inserted in its present location by some accident in the process of copying. Certainly the contents agree with the hint Paul furnishes to the contents of his first letter.

How could such an accident have occurred?

The letters in the possession of the various churches were kept in the "church box," which seems to have been a large chest. In most instances the writing was done on large squares of papyrus paper. In some cases these leaves were glued together to make a long strip, which was rolled up. In other cases they were bound together like a book. Then, of course, there may have been some loose leaves in the church boxes whereon were written brief letters. When we think how common it is today to slip a clipping inside a book for safekeeping, it is easy to imagine that a single letter on a single sheet might have been slipped into a longer letter; and when some copyist reproduced them later, he naturally assumed that they were all of one piece.

Was this not careless handling of scripture?

At this point we must remember that Paul's letters were not esteemed to be scripture by the churches to which they were addressed. They were wise and devout messages from their trusted leader and as such were accorded very great respect. It was believed that he had written them under the pressure of the Holy Spirit, but that they were "inspired scripture" as the Old Testament was neither Paul nor the early Christians seemed to think. Rather they were treasured in some such fashion as we treasure old hymns. All Christians recognize that God has moved upon the minds of the hymn writers, but no one would feel that there was any dishonesty or sacrilege involved in changing a word or a line of some old composition, if by such a change we could make it express a great spiritual truth to better advantage.

159 What can we believe about the matter, then?

Certainly there is no positive proof that this small section of Second Corinthians (6:14–7:1) is the lost letter; but it could be, for it fits Paul's description, and, as we shall discover a little later, it is known that more than one book is included in the book called Second Corinthians.

160 What about the letter Paul received from Corinth?

As has been stated, the letter seems to have contained a series of questions upon which the Corinthian church sought Paul's advice. It was brought by the committee, who expected to carry the answer back with them. They must have discussed these matters at some length with the man who founded their church and who was responsible for whatever knowledge they had of the Christian way.

161 What were those questions?

We must guess at their form, basing our judgment upon Paul's reply, but there seem to have been at least six questions.

162 What was the first question they asked?

It must have related in some way to the question of marriage. What is the Christian idea of marriage? Is it wrong to marry? What about divorce? Shall betrothed people proceed to marry? The first question was evidently of some such form.

163 How did Paul answer the question?

He insisted that the Christians must separate themselves from the immorality of the city, and this raised the question as to whether a Christian must separate himself from an un-Christian mate. Should a Christian give his daughter in marriage to an unconverted youth? Should a Christian ever marry a heathen? Even more to the point was the question as to whether those intending to marry should proceed to do so. In answering these questions Paul was deeply influenced by two factors: (1) his Jewish training and background, and (2) his belief that Jesus would return speedily. The standards of the Jews in the matter

58

of the marriage relation were very much higher than those of the Greeks, and Paul insisted upon this higher standard. At the same time the Jews accorded less freedom to women, and Paul reflected that opinion. Then, because of his belief that Jesus would put in his appearance at any time, he believed that all questions of marriage should be set aside unless individuals found it necessary to marry in order to restrain their physical passions (7:25-40). These decisions sound like strange doctrines, but they were put forth only as restrictions to operate "until the Lord shall come." At that time an entirely new type of life would be established.

164 What was the second question?

This also will sound strange to modern ears, but to the Corinthians it was a very real problem: Where should they buy their meat? It was a pagan custom to offer animal sacrifices to the gods. By killing an animal and offering its blood to the god a certain divine favor was secured. But more to the point, and perhaps more practical, was the fact that once the blood was offered to the god the meat became available to the public as food, being sold by the temple authorities. As a matter of religious practice the animals so offered were always the fattest and choicest, and this meant that the best cuts of meat were purchased at the shrines. The average Christian probably bought such meat without raising any moral questions. But among the Christians there were those who had the feeling that to eat such meat was to sanction idolatry in some way, and the issue had become acute inside the church. Were they, by buying such meat, disclaiming their new-found Lord? The profits from the shrines—and the sale of meat—went to help support the pagan religion and all its horrid practices and just as the question of buying groceries from a store that also sells liquor is a problem in the minds of some modern Christians, so this problem of buying meat was a problem in the minds of some ancient Christians.

165 How did Paul solve the meat problem?

There were two views on this subject among Christians, each of which was stoutly defended. One group insisted that such eating of meat involved no moral question, that it implied no endorsement of idolatry. The other group suffered from a sensitive conscience on the subject. The two viewpoints are summed up in chapter 8. In chapters 9 and 10 Paul explains his own position in some detail. If eating meat which has been offered to idols is to impose a temptation on another Christian, then he will eat no meat under any circumstances. Here is one of the highest ethical and moral positions taken by any writer in the New Testament.

166 What was the third question?

It was the question of whether or not women should wear veils when they attended the Christian services of worship.

Greek married women were not allowed any part in public affairs, though courtesans were, and so any Greek woman who appeared in a public place without a veil was taken for a courtesan. Jewish women, although they enjoyed more freedom in many ways, were subject to an even more rigid sex and moral code.

Christian meetings, for the most part, were held inside private homes, where normally a woman might have expected to enjoy greater liberties. The question, then, was: Should a woman attending a Christian service inside a private house dress as if she were attending a public meeting, or more as if she were a personal and private guest of the home? The whole issue sounds trivial to us, but to the infant Church it had become very important.

167 How did Paul solve the problem?

Here again Paul's early training obtruded itself. It was very difficult for him to surrender his old prejudices, and at this point in his letter he probably reaches his lowest level. He insists that the women, contrary to the principle of equality of the sexes in Christ which he had declared in theory (Galatians 3:28), must wear veils in worship, for to expose their heads like men seemed to Paul indecent (I Corinthians 11:5).

168 What was the fourth question in dispute?

This is one with which we are somewhat more familiar. What about the extravagances known as "speaking in tongues"? Under the spell of great emotion Christians here and there broke out into an incoherent babble which no one could understand. It became infectious, and soon the meetings were wild and disorderly. There were those who believed these manifestations were evidence of the emphatic presence of the Holy Spirit, but they were working havoc with the Christian movement and making the church a by-word in the city. What should they do?

169 What did Paul have to say on that subject?

He admits that he had himself spoken in tongues on a few occasions (14:2-8, 18), but he assures the Corinthians that he thinks the gift of tongues is the lowest form of spiritual expression. Instead of seeking the gift, he urges them to believe in the higher graces and to cultivate the better spiritual gifts (12:31); and with that he launches out into a description of Christian love in a prose poem which is, without question, the finest literary gem in all his writings (chap. 13).

The gift of tongues has long been associated with religious enthusiasm, especially among primitive people and those who are highly emotional. It is not limited to Christians, but is reported as occurring also among savages in the jungle in connection with primitive rites. The individual who exercises the gift speaks a gibberish that is unintelligible to the hearers, and also to himself. Thus the "speaking" is entirely without benefit to anyone, except as it may incite some wonder or gratify some vanity. The only effect is the bewilderment of those who witness it and a confusion in the mind of the one who "speaks." He usually takes pride in the fact that he has been visited by the Spirit of God, in spite of the fact that he is unable to recall afterward anything he has said or the meaning thereof. This peculiar phenomenon appeared quite frequently among the Christians of the first century and gave rise to no small embarrassment. Modern psychology understands the matter very well, but the limitations of our space do not permit us to go into any detailed explanation. Suffice it to say that Paul regarded it as the lowest expression of spirituality and warned all men against seeking it.

170 What was the fifth question?

This has to do with the resurrection of the dead, concerning which there was much misunderstanding.

In this connection we find Paul at his best. There were two ideas of immortality abroad in the world. The Greeks believed in it as an existence entirely separate from the body. The soul, they believed, would somehow float free from the body, which was thought to be an impediment, and enter into a larger life that would be eternal. Concerning just what that life was to be like they were not very clear, but at least they were convinced that it had no physical connections. The Jews, on the other hand, could not think of any life apart from the body. If a soul did exist apart from the body, it was no more than a shade or a ghost, without actual existence, and without any means of self-expression or self-realization. To the Hebrew, then, any resurrection involved a reunion of the spirit and the body.

In answering the Corinthian question Paul takes a position about midway between that of the Greeks and that of the Jews, though it is evident that he leans toward the Jewish concept. He says that the soul will have a body, but that it will not be such a body as the one with which we are familiar, rather some sort of ethereal or spiritual body which will suffice for self-expression and not interfere with spiritual expression. He seemed to believe that Jesus had risen from the grave and had been clothed with some sort of exquisite matter, something like light. He remembered, or course, the vision he had seen on the Damascus way. But the central element in Paul's doctrine was his conviction that the individual would continue as an independent spiritual identity, and would not be absorbed into the "universal soul" of which some Greek thinkers discoursed. All this he describes in some detail in chapter 15, one of the most profound writings in all his letters.

172
What was the sixth question?

This involved the matter of settling disputes between Christians. Though they were supposed to be united in a fellowship, trouble had developed between individuals, and they had taken their cases into the courts, thus making their Christian professions a laughing stock in the city.

173
What about those lawsuits?

In order that the pagans might not get a wrong impression of the Christians, seeing them in the courts settling their differences, Paul made a very earnest appeal that they should find some way of adjusting disputes without resort to law (6:1-8). How are they to save the world, he asks, if they cannot settle simple matters between themselves? It is still good advice.

174 When was this letter written?

It is believed that Paul left Corinth about A.D. 54 and that this letter was written three years afterward?

175 What picture do we get of the Corinthian church?

It was made up of Corinthians. As they assemble, we may see people of all classes come together—former adulterers, dissipaters, fornicators, drunkards, thieves, slaves, freemen, extortioners, the lewd, and the lascivious. Never was such an experiment made as when Paul tried to produce a Christian church out of such material. They were mostly ignorant, unschooled, untrained, and deficient people. That was the miracle. They were far from perfect, but they had caught a vision of perfection in Jesus.

176 What significance does all this have?

There has been a tendency among modern Christians to assume that these ancients were perfect models of Christianity, full of grace and altogether without fault. We cannot rejoice, of course, that they fell short of those standards, but it should be a source of encouragement to us to know that God used such a church, composed as it was of people who fell so far short of perfection. Perhaps he can use the modern Church also in spite of its imperfections.

177 But there are two letters to the Corinthians.

As a matter of fact we have at least three letters to the Corinthians in the New Testament, and we know that Paul wrote at least one other.

178 What is Second Corinthians?

It is some more of Paul's personal correspondence with the church at Corinth, in which two greatly differing moods are reflected. This raises an extremely interesting question.

179   What is the question?

Second Corinthians opens with nine chapters that are all "sweetness and light." They breathe a spirit of good will and graciousness. Occasional phrases sound almost apologetic. Then suddenly the tenth chapter changes climate. Paul seems highly indignant over personal affronts and defends himself stoutly against charges of inefficiency and misconduct.

180   What is the reason for this?

Careful students have come to the conclusions that the book actually consists of two different letters. It is known, for instance, that all such communications were delivered by a personal messenger, and it is hardly probable that Paul would have sent two such contradictory messages in the same letter. The first nine chapters are conciliatory and the last four severe to the last degree. The Corinthian church may have combined the two letters for use in the public worship services, somewhat as we combine psalms in our responsive readings, or they may have been combined by some accident.

181   What is the explanation of the two messages?

Paul's second letter (I Corinthians) seems to have failed in its purpose; the factions continued and grew worse. To correct them, and to answer certain charges leveled against him, Paul wrote another letter (believed to be II Corinthians 10–13) and sent it by the hand of Titus, a trusted colleague. It is quite possible that the personal word of Titus helped the Corinthians to get Paul's viewpoint; and when he returned to Paul, he was able to report a restored church and a renewed confidence in Paul. This resulted in another letter, of gracious good will and conciliation.

182   What is our final conclusion?

The student may want to take an inexpensive New Testament, cut it up, and rearrange it so that the various portions are in their chronological order. He may even want to rename the letters:

First Letter to the Corinthians—II 6:14–7:1
Second Letter to the Corinthians—I, complete
Third Letter to the Corinthians—II 10–13

Fourth Letter to the Corinthians—II 1–9 (except 6:14–7:1)

183 How had Paul's second letter failed?

As has been suggested, the factions increased in bitterness. Those opposed to Paul agreed upon only one thing—they refused to accept his leadership. The church was on the verge of a complete rupture.

184 What was Paul's reaction?

He was deeply stirred. In writing of the circumstances sometime later in his final letter, he says he was so crushed he actually despaired of his life (1:8 f.). He may even have made them a visit while in this state of mind (2:1). But at least we know he wrote them a letter (2:3 f.) which was so strong that he wound up regretting having sent it (7:8). This letter having gone forward by the hand of Titus, Paul set out for Troas expecting Titus to join him there with news of the effect produced at Corinth; but in this he seems to have been disappointed (2:13). It is because in the last four chapters of Second Corinthians we have exactly the kind of letter he might have written under such circumstances, that many scholars believe they are the letter.

185 What about those four chapters?

They constitute the boldest, most straightforward writing we have from the pen of Paul in all the New Testament. Moreover they are more biographical than anything else we have, supplying considerable information concerning Paul which is to be found nowhere else in the New Testament. In fact, there is so much of the personal element in these chapters that, unless we understand the circumstances which produced them, it is easy to think them little less than shameless boasting. Instead of employing his usual modest, kindly style, Paul writes almost viciously at times. With fine indignation he rebukes the Christians of Corinth for misconstruing his work and words. He dares them to point out any real fault in his authority. With fine scorn he warns them against listening to any superfine apostles (11:5, 13), and reminds them that his policy of self-support was adopted in their behalf. With a keen understanding of human nature he reminds them that no matter what he would have done they would have found fault. Thereupon he sets out to outboast them all.

Only in Second Corinthians do we get an adequate picture of the hardships through which he passed in the course of his career (11:24-28). In addition, there is the record of his spiritual experiences. Acts tells the story of the experience on the Damascus Road (Acts 9:1-15), but Second Corinthians tells of additional visions (12:1-11) of an unusual nature. Acts tells of the animosities of the Jews, but Second Corinthians draws the curtain back and allows us to see the opposition which developed inside the Church itself.

187 Why was there opposition to Paul in the Corinthian church?

It seems that preachers from Jerusalem—perhaps the same ones who had also disturbed the work in Galatia—appeared in Corinth claiming superior authority for their apostleship and making some trouble for Paul (11:5). Either they or members of the Corinthian church under their influence began making petty personal criticisms. The situation sounds very much like a modern church quarrel. They said Paul was unimpressive in personal appearance (10:10). Besides this trivial accusation—which has been leveled at many a modern preacher—they drew contemptuous conclusions from his financial policy. In this they were different from some modern pulpit committees that accuse the minister of "preaching for money." They reversed the charge and found fault with him because he did not take payment for his services (11:7-9).

188 Why was this considered a fault?

The Corinthians judged all wandering preachers by the way they commercialized their calling. The more pretentious lecturers in halls charged big fees, but Paul accepted no money in any amount. This gave him the standing of a soap-box orator.

189 What other charges were there?

Only the one criticism about his appearance is quoted verbatim (10:10), but we can judge of the others by Paul's replies in this third letter and also by references in his fourth letter, after the trouble was settled. Paul defends himself against at least five charges.

190 What were they?

1. His personal appearance was poor—10:10
2. His speech was uncouth—11:6
3. He was only a nobody—12:11
4. He taught an obscure doctrine—4:3
5. He was fickle and unreliable—1:15-17

191 What does Paul say about his personal appearance?

He makes no direct reply, perhaps feeling the criticism is beneath his notice, but he does suggest that a man should be judged by his spirit rather than by his personal appearance (10:7; 11:14). Others may glory in their physical appearance, but he prefers to glory in the gospel of Christ. He does make the observation, however, that God's power is sometimes revealed more perfectly in weakness than in strength (12:9-10), but this may have been a reference to his infirmity.

192 What was that infirmity?

It is impossible to speak exactly about it, for all we know is that after experiencing his visions he suffered from some terrible agony which he called a "thorn in the flesh." In spite of prayers for deliverance it had continued, and finally he came to think of it as a badge of honor (12:7-10). Modern psychologists have suggested that he may have suffered from some type of epilepsy, but of this there can be no proof. Others with some plausibility suggest eye trouble.

193 What does he say about the uncouth speech?

In his earlier letter (I Corinthians) Paul declared very frankly that he had avoided all tricks of the professional orator in order that he might speak plainly. He had not set out to tickle their ears, but to speak plain truths (2:1, 4), and it had to be admitted that he had got results (2:4) and that God had used him as a preacher of the new faith (3:6). Now, in answer to specific criticism, he says that his shortcomings as a speaker are made up for by his sincerity and the certainty of his knowledge of the truth he preaches (10:10, 11:6).

194 What does he say about his unimportance?

In First Corinthians he spoke humbly of his experiences (15:8

f.). The faultfinders evidently construed this as a weakness, for Paul hints they were calling him a nobody (II 11:16; 12:11). Now, putting aside his humility, he boasts that he is "not in the least inferior to these superlative apostles" (11:5; 12:11). He claims his authority from the Lord (10:8). He points proudly to his birth and heritage (11:22), his labors and sufferings for Christ (11:23-27), his concern over the churches and their members (11:28 f.), and his visions (12:1-5). And in his later letter he adds a few further words in defense of his claim to be equal with any other apostles. Though he lacks credentials from Jerusalem, his converts are his credentials (3:1-3). Though he has not known Jesus in the flesh, neither does anyone else walk with Christ in the flesh since he is risen (5:16). By this line of reasoning he established the right of all Christians to witness to the faith. There was to be no spiritual aristocracy inside the Church.

195 What does he say about the obscurity of his doctrine?

Evidently Paul's doctrine seemed mysterious to the Corinthians from the start (I 2:7). Now some have complained and doubted its authenticity (II 13:3). Paul, who is expecting to come in person soon (13:1), refrains from argument about it in a letter, except to attack the "false apostles" who have contradicted him (11:4, 11-15). Later, probably prevented from making the visit, he thinks it wise in his conciliatory letter to deny specific charges—that he has corrupted the word of God (2:17), that he has handled it deceitfully (4:2), and that he has preached about himself and not Christ (4:5).

196 What does he say about the charges against his character?

At this point Paul becomes vehement. He does not resent the questions about his personal appearance very seriously, but he does become indignant when his integrity is questioned. They have said he thunders at them from a distance but dares not face them in person, thus inferring that his letters are an evasion of his duty to visit them. In reply he denies that he has used violent or unworthy methods or sought his own glory, and reminds them that God has used him (10:3-9); but he declares that he will show them plenty of vigor when he does come (10:11; 13:2). Then, after finding the visit impractical, he assures them that his frequent changes of plans, for which they have charged him with fickleness, were not a weakness but a desire to spare them (1:23).

197 What was the effect of this vehement letter?

Paul sent the letter by the hand of his friend Titus with instructions that the reply was to be delivered back to Troas. Considerable delay ensued, and Titus did not arrive. Paul went on to Macedonia, and there Titus met him with the good news that the Corinthians had changed their attitude completely (7:5-7), and for a time he was almost repentant that he had written such a letter (2:4; 7:8). Titus reported that they were now directing their energies against the troublemakers, and were anxious for Paul to visit them that they might reassure him of their loyalty.

198 What was Paul's reaction?

He was greatly relieved, of course, and sat down to write them another letter.

199 What about that letter?

No longer under the necessity of defending his position, he shows a warm affection for the Corinthians, and even intercedes for the trouble-makers. As in the preceding letter he had given free rein to his indignation, in this letter he pours out his heart in an endearing tide.

200 Had there been any justification for the Corinthian charges?

There may have been some small justification. The Corinthians had written Paul a letter, and this he had barely acknowledged in his reply (I Corinthians). Instead he had upbraided them on the basis of the report he had from Chloe's people, which was, in effect, hearsay evidence. It must be admitted that he proceeded against them pretty vigorously, telling them he was coming after them with a stick (4:21) as if they were little children. He assured them that they were not the only church in the world, even though they did have a good opinion of themselves (11:16; 14:33-36). He even told them he had to treat them like babies (1:26; 3:1). The general severity of

69

his language (4:7; 5:1; 6:1-11; 11:17, 22) was such that at least the Corinthians can be understood if they resented it.

201 Did Paul think he was writing scripture in these letters?

It was a human situation which called for rare spiritual discernment, and Paul's experience had given him the solution. He does not suggest that he was writing any mysterious message which required special illumination, but because of the wholesomeness of judgments the book has become scripture.

202 What is the message of this fourth letter?

In the first place, it opens with a profound expression of gratitude for the happy outcome of the whole matter. In one paragraph of five verses (II 1:3-7) he uses the word "comfort" in some form or other ten times, and introduces the idea in later passages (7:6, 7, 13). As though he wants all the world to know that the dispute between him and the Corinthian church is at an end, he addresses the Christians of all Greece (1:1-2). In order to smooth matters over he reviews the entire case in gentle tones (1:12-14) and apologizes for his inability to visit them (1:15–2:3) and for his harsh letter (2:4). In one of his finest passages he defines his motives and methods as a missionary (2:12–6:10), and expresses complete confidence in the restored relationship (7:5-16). With these matters settled, he proceeds to the collection.

203 What about the collection?

There was a sharp division between the Jerusalem Christians and the Greek converts who had come into the fellowship in such large numbers through the ministry of Paul. The Jewish Christians were slow about welcoming the Greeks, for they still thought of the Christian movement as something inside Judaism. Paul was attempting to bridge the gulf between the two groups, and when a famine struck Palestine it seemed to play directly into his hands. He began collecting funds from the Gentile Christians for the purpose of relieving the distress among the Jerusalem Christians.

204 How successful was he?

We have no exact knowledge of the results, though there is

good reason to believe that the Corinthian church joined with the others in a good collection. We know that Paul made a trip to Jerusalem for the purpose of turning the funds over to the Christian leaders.

205 What was the later history of the Corinthian church?

There is little in the New Testament to give us any light. The writings of the Church Fathers of the first few centuries indicate that it continued to be a strong organization for many years. But the city fell into ruins in the course of time as a result of political upheavals, and by the middle of the nineteenth century it was only a small Greek city of about 10,000 souls, as it is today. But Paul's letters, containing nothing but words, have outlasted stones, walls, and commerce. And in them we have one very unusual bit of writing.

206 What is that unusual bit of writing?

We shall learn when we come to a study of the four Gospels, the "lives" of Jesus which profess to give us much information concerning him, that they were actually written after Paul's letters to the churches. Therefore the bit of record found in First Corinthians 11:23-26 and 15:3-9, telling of the Last Supper and the Resurrection, is the earliest written record of any act or event in the life of our Lord which is to be found anywhere in the world. The scientific student of these two subjects will start with Paul's letter to the Corinthians rather than with the four Gospels.

207 What was Paul's next letter?

There seems to be general agreement that it was the letter to the Romans.

208 Was there a Christian church in Rome?

There was, and a vigorous one at that. When Paul sat down to write his letter to the Christians there, they enjoyed a great reputation throughout the world (Romans 1:8).

209 Did Paul found the church at Rome?

No. When he wrote his letter to the Roman church, he had

perhaps never seen any Roman Christians except Aquila and Priscilla, by whom he was employed in Corinth (Acts 18:2).

210 Who founded the Roman church?

History throws little light on this subject. The Roman Catholic Church claims Peter did, but the evidence is not accepted by Protestants. We know that, following the death of Stephen by stoning, the Christians in Jerusalem who were natives of other sections of the empire scattered widely, and they doubtless carried their message to their home communities. It seems reasonable to believe that some such may have started the church in Rome, and that Peter preached to the Christians there at an early date (see Acts 11:19).

211 Was there some difficulty in the Roman church?

In this respect the letter to the Romans is unique. In the case of other letters the reason for writing was the correction of some difficulty, but in the case of the letter to the Romans the cause was personal and related to Paul's plans.

212 What was Paul's personal problem?

His missionary work in the East was done. There were communities which he might have visited, but twenty-five years of preaching had seen growing churches established in all the great centers. His interests now turned to the West, beyond Rome, to Spain. He had designs upon the world and was laying plans to plant Christian churches throughout the empire. But an immediate responsibility made it impossible. He must go to Jerusalem.

213 Why was Spain so important?

The Western world was just opening up. It occupied something of the same relationship to the empire in Paul's day as the West sustained to the United States following the War Between the States. Great strides were being made in learning and culture. Men like Seneca, Martial, Lucan, and Quintillian—all from the West—were becoming famous throughout the learned circles of the empire. Very clearly Spain was the coming country and Christianity's next great opportunity.

214   What called Paul to Jerusalem?

A cleavage was beginning to appear in the Christian ranks. Healing this breach was Paul's first obligation?

215   What was this cleavage?

It revolved about the question of the Greek Christians, who were in the vast majority. Whereas the Jerusalem church consisted of only a small group of Christians, the Greek wing consisted of congregations in scores of cities and towns. It is impossible to reckon in terms of exact statistics, but the Greeks must have outnumbered the Jews by many thousands. Yet the Jerusalem church was reckoned as the leader, and in some respects the final authority in the movement.

216   What was Paul's relationship to this situation?

Throughout the Church he was recognized as the leader of the Greek wing of the movement, and if Greek congregations were to be held in line, Paul was the man who could do it. But the root of the trouble was not among the Greeks; it stemmed from the attitude of the Jerusalem church. The Christians there had never surrendered the conviction that all Greeks should become Jews before they could become Christians. While preaching among the Greeks, Paul had devised a plan which he hoped would heal the breach between the two sections.

217   What was Paul's plan?

The collection.

218   How many collections did Paul take?

We have a record of his having gathered two collections for the suffering Christians. The first was gathered very early in his career as a preacher (Acts 11:27-30), but the one usually referred to in speaking of Paul's collection is the one he gathered toward the close of his public ministry, concerning which we are studying.

219   From whom did Paul collect the money?

From all the Greek churches, but extended mention is made in Paul's fourth letter to the Corinthians (II Corinthians 9), and the congregations of Galatia, Asia, Macedonia, and Greece seem to have shared in the enterprise (Romans 15:26; II Corinthians 8:3, 6; 9:2; 1 Corinthians 16:1).

220 Why did Paul have to take it in person to Jerusalem?

It would not have been necessary for Paul to go in person in order to deliver the funds, for the banking system of the day was quite competent to transfer letters of credit. But the mere transfer of money was not enough. The significance of the collection had to be explained, and its spiritual results had to be conserved. Paul wanted the collection to do more than merely relieve physical distress among the Jerusalem Christians. He also wanted it to heal a breach between the Greeks and the Jews in the Christian movement, and this could not be done unless Paul visited Jerusalem in person and made a direct appeal.

221 Did this need to delay him seriously?

Two hazards entered the scene. In the first place, it was well known that Jerusalem was seething with discontent, and that Rome was watching the city very carefully. Only ten years later the Jews rose in revolt and brought down upon their heads the terrible wrath of the empire. No one knew what might happen in Palestine and Jerusalem; the city was the empire's number one danger zone. In the second place, no one could be absolutely sure what the reactions of the Jerusalem Christians might be. Extremists from among them had gone up into Galatia and Corinth in a studied effort to interfere with Paul's work among the Gentiles and had returned discomfited. It was entirely possible that Paul might find them unrelenting in their attitudes in spite of any collection. He had had to deal severely with them in both Corinth and in Galatia, and no one knew what resentment they might cherish or what reports they may have brought back to Jerusalem concerning him.

222 Where was Paul in the meantime?

He was spending the winter in Corinth, toward which city the delegates were converging, bringing the collection. One or two from each congregation were appointed to make the journey with him, and these were to carry the funds (Acts 20:4).

223 When was the trip made?

We cannot speak with exactness on this point, for the records are inadequate, but the delegates must have begun to assemble toward the close of the year 57. They probably set out for Jerusalem soon after the Mediterranean was opened to navigation in the spring of 58.

224 What did Paul decide to do in the case of the Romans?

He postponed his trip to visit them and wrote a letter.

225 What did he hope to accomplish with a letter?

He had never had a chance to preach to the Romans, or to instruct them in the Christian faith. It had always been his rule to avoid those centers where other men had preached and organized a church (Romans 15:20; II Corinthians 10:16). He knew that the Roman church could not be more than half instructed under the circumstances, and he felt it necessary to explain to them the great basic doctrines and ideas. If he could not preach to them in person, a careful statement of his position put down in writing would be the next best thing. Even more, he wanted to inform the Roman church of his plans for a Spanish campaign. They were the congregation farthest west and very naturally had a deep interest in pushing the frontiers farther out. It was very necessary, then, that Paul should have the support of the church at his back as he went out to Spain.

226 Was there any theological controversy in the Roman church?

None so far as we know. They were not the victims of any heretical teaching, they were rent by no dissension, there was no gross immorality being practiced among them. But they were only half trained, and it could not be hoped that they would go forever undisturbed.

227 In what respect is his letter to the Romans different?

In the case of his letter to the Corinthians, for instance, it was not necessary for him to go into the whole question of his theology and to state his position on a great variety of matters.

He had preached among them and had taught them thoroughly on at least a few subjects, and his letters were needed only to clear up some remaining points. But in the case of the Romans, whom he had never met, and who had never heard him expound the faith, it was necessary to make a more or less complete statement of his entire position. This called for an entirely different style of writing.

228 How does Romans differ in style?

It is restrained, conservative in statement, careful in the choice of words, and logical in its arrangement. Paul was addressing the church in the capital of the world and was endeavoring to make a statement of faith which might serve as something like an official text for the entire Christian movement. This made it a missionary book.

229 What is its missionary message?

Paul believed that Christianity had a message for the whole world which was quite independent of Jewish forms and Jewish laws. It was to him a new religion with a spiritual dynamic all its own and a universal message. By a tortuous pilgrimage he had arrived at the place where he proposed to teach Christ, quite apart from any Jewish implications, as the world's hope of salvation. In doing so he coveted the assistance of the church at Rome, and in his epistle to the Romans he appealed for their support in the propagation of this universal message.

230 What is the unique characteristic of the book?

Its spirit of universality. It believes strongly in a universal salvation for a civilization that is universally in need. The world was Paul's great concern, and all people were members of his parish. In addition, there are a number of peculiarities in the book.

231 What are some of these peculiarities?

There are over sixty quotations from the Old Testament in Romans—more than in all the other Pauline epistles combined. The phrase "as it is written" occurs nineteen times. Life after death is declared as a belief, but is in no way described. The word "hell" does not appear in the book at all, but the word "heaven" appears twice. There is no allusion to the cross, though mention is made of the death of Christ; and the Resurrection—central in much of Paul's preaching—gets less attention than in Corinthians. Little or nothing is said about the person of Christ, and the Church is scarcely mentioned. The only personal matters are cases in which Paul seems to be trying to clear up some misunderstandings or misquotations (3:8, 31; 6:1, 15; 7:7). Perhaps the most puzzling thing in the letter is the sixteenth chapter.

232 What about the sixteenth chapter?

This is a letter of introduction for a woman named Phoebe, one of the deaconesses of the church at Cenchreae, who is about to make a journey. Greetings are extended to twenty-six people, all of whom are Paul's personal friends and acquaintances. Among those mentioned are Aquila and Prisca (Priscilla in Acts), who seem to have fled from Rome some years before as a result of a persecution of the Jews. They are first mentioned in the New Testament as having established themselves in the tentmaking business in Corinth, where they employed Paul (Acts 18:1-3). Later they removed to Ephesus (Acts 18:18 f., 26), where they again engaged in business, and where they became leading figures in the Ephesian church. The long list of names in Romans 16 indicates that Paul must have had a very wide circle of friends; and this would have been true in Ephesus, for he had labored there through a period of some two years (Acts 19:8-10). The warning against disobeying his instructions (Romans 16:17) sounds strange if it is directed at the Romans, with whom he has not previously been in contact. This and other reasons encourage many scholars to believe this last chapter is a separate letter which was addressed to the church at Ephesus as an introduction for Phoebe. Years afterward the Ephesian church made a collection of Paul's letters and seems to have attached this to the letter to the Romans, perhaps for convenience' sake. There is little value in it except as it gives us a glimpse at the personnel of the early Church.

233 Was the Roman church a Gentile church?

It appears that Greeks, Jews, and Romans were to be found in the membership of the church at Rome. At one time Paul addresses himself to the Jews (2:17-24; 7:1), and at other times he addresses the Gentiles (1:5-7, 13). Rome was a city of about 1,500,000 people, of which number probably 50,000 were Jews.

They had a number of synagogues in the city, and their community life was well organized, for Paul had no difficulty in getting in touch with their leaders when he arrived in chains some two years afterward (Acts 28:17) to await trial. When Paul wrote his letter to the Roman church, the Jews were well entrenched in the business and artistic life of the capital.

234 What do we learn about the life of the Roman church?

In chapter 14 Paul discusses the two groups which have formed inside the church. One seems to have laid great emphasis on the Jewish observances, but Paul's sympathies were with the liberal group, though he makes a strong plea that the scruples of the stricter sect shall be respected. This sounds as if there might have been some friction in the church. Elsewhere in the letter (chaps. 9-11) Paul pleads with the Gentile members in behalf of the Jewish members of the congregation, which again seems to indicate the existence of some sort of friction, but concerning its precise nature we know nothing.

235 Does Paul furnish us any personal information in this letter?

Much concerning Paul comes from chapter 15 (vv. 14-33), wherein he describes his plan for his western missionary campaign. There is an extended section (12:1–15:13) which outlines a Christian's duties as a servant of the state and a member of the Church.

236 What does Paul have to say about the state?

No one knew better than Paul did what the ruthlessness of the empire was like. He must have been well aware of the possibility of a clash between the state and the Church. This he hoped, if possible, to avoid. As a Roman citizen he was loyal to the empire, and as a Christian he was determined that the Church should not run afoul of the law. The state, in his opinion, was an agent of God so long as it maintained order, and it was the duty of the Christians to support the state in that matter. As a question of prudence, as well as of conscience, he urged obedience to law and submission to authority (chap. 13).

What about chapters 1-11?

After a careful and ingratiating introduction (1:1-13), in which he apologizes for the fact that he has not visited them earlier, Paul announces his mission to the Greek and the Jew, and then in 1:17 lays down his great theme: "He who through faith is righteous shall live." These words taken from Habakkuk (2:4) meant, on the lips of the Old Testament prophet, "The upright shall survive because of their steadfastness"; but to Paul they meant, "He who is righteous in the sense that he has faith will obtain life." From this point on the Apostle undertakes to show that men are saved by faith, and that faith has been made possible by the death of Christ. The wisdom of the Gentiles (1:18-2:11)—by which he means philosophy—and the Law of the Jews (2:12-3:20) are equally futile. But faith is within the reach of Jew and Gentile (3:21-31). The Jews called themselves the "children of Abraham," believing they are the inheritors of the promise made to the patriarch; but Paul points out that Abraham's virtue was not his physical nature but his religious faith, and declares that the man in whose veins the blood of Abraham flows is no more the heir of the promise than the one who is faithful (chap. 4) and is therefore a spiritual child of Abraham. Then follow four chapters (5-8) which discuss the question of salvation from sin. Paul believed that Christ in anyone's life produced an entirely new set of motives, a new kind of life, purer desires, and a more spiritual type of moral energy. The believer with faith is lifted out of the old life (chaps. 7-8). The three final chapters of this argument (9-11), having to do with the destiny of Israel, are vague and difficult to understand because we do not know enough about the conditions existing in the Roman church.

What is our final impression of Paul from these letters?

After a hurried journey through nine of Paul's letters while he was yet a free man, we find something very inspiring about the figure of the little tentmaker who hurried from one great city to another, earning his living as a craftsman and preaching in his spare hours, all the while planning a conquest of the world. Beset by perils of every description, misrepresented by his enemies, misunderstood by his friends, striving with might and main to hold Jew and Greek together in a common fellowship, writing letters that are to form the foundations of a new religion, the converted Pharisee has become the world's greatest thinker and evangelist. As he starts his letter on its way to the Romans and heads for Jerusalem, we have a presentiment that a great tragedy is awaiting him. It is with this same foreboding that he penned his last lines to the church at Rome (15:31-32).